...yone...
...terature...
...ns sure to appeal to the reader in your life.

LeVar Burton, *Reading Rainbow*

I know I'm not the only one who's stood in the middle of the children's section at the library or bookstore knowing I'm surrounded by good books to read but wishing someone would point me toward which ones to choose—and which to pass over. Now Jamie is here to help me do just that. She's done the hard work of sorting the good stuff from the mediocre, highlighting her family's favorite titles region by region. Now I'm free to focus on the fun part: reading good books with my kids.

Anne Bogel, blogger at Modern Mrs. Darcy

I've traveled all over the globe and have seen both amazingly beautiful and horrifically tragic parts of our planet. I want my children to impact and alleviate the world's hurts one day, but first they have to fall in love with it. That's where a resource like Jamie's book comes in. It enables our families to read our way to a love for the world, thereby giving fuel to our determination to heal it in the unique way God created us to.

Christine Caine, founder of the A21 Campaign

Give Your Child the World is a must-read for every parent who wants to expand their child's worldview beyond the suburban bubble of middle-class American culture. Can't afford to travel? Jamie proves that giving your children cross-cultural experiences need not cost a dime. A library card and a strong imagination can make it happen!

Erin Odom, creator of TheHumbledHomemaker.com and upcoming author with HarperCollins Christian Publishing

Give Your Child the World is an absolutely brilliant book. I love how Jamie has taken carefully selected literature from all over and about the world, broken it into topics, countries, and age ranges, and created an incredible resource where I can simply open the pages and choose. It's also filled with practical ideas and inspiration to help me teach my children about the beauty and diversity of the world. She's done the work! I can't wait to get started "traveling" the world!

Sarah Mae, author of *Having a Martha Home the Mary Way*

For parents who want their children to fall in love with the world, right from the coziness of home. Jamie knows that stories are the most powerful way to reach the heart of a child, and this collection of carefully selected books will be a worthy companion for mindful parents everywhere. A treasure trove!

Sarah Mackenzie, creator of the *Read-Aloud Revival* podcast and online community; author of *Teaching from Rest: A Homeschooler's Guide to Unshakable Peace*

In the day-in, day-out craziness of life, I have this nagging feeling that I should be teaching my kids about the whole wide world, but I have no idea how. Jamie Martin has done all the hard work for us in *Give Your Child the World*. What a resource! This book is chock-full of creative ideas and book suggestions to lead our families around the globe without ever leaving our homes. Every parent needs a copy.

Melanie Dale, author of *Women Are Scary: The Totally Awkward Adventure of Finding Mom Friends* and *It's Not Fair: Learning to Love the Life You Didn't Choose*

Inspiring, accessible, and supremely practical, *Give Your Child the World* is an outstanding resource for families who want their children to engage the world and shape its future. It helps children imagine, believe, and love. *Give Your Child the World* makes dreams tangible for children. We highly recommend it!

Stephan Bauman, president of World Relief and author of *Possible: A Blueprint for Changing How We Change the World*—and Belinda Bauman, author, educator, and founder of One Million Thumbprints

The world is smaller than ever and only getting smaller. As parents, we would do well to raise our children so they are able to navigate the increasingly global society they will live in. Jamie has given us parents an incredible gift. With practical ideas and a wonderful reading list, *Give Your Child the World* is a valuable resource in raising compassionate, global-minded kids who love the whole world.

Nate Pyle, pastor, blogger, and author of *Man Enough*

As parents, we have a deep desire to raise our kids with cultural sensitivity and awareness. So much so that we've made traveling around the world as a family a priority, to give our kids rich cultural experiences that we hope will shape them into adults who make a difference. I only wish I'd had Jamie's amazing book before we started traveling, to help me find books for our kids to read in preparation for the places we visited. But even better, I think it's the perfect tool for those who aren't able to travel. Stories are one of the best ways to develop empathy, compassion, and gain someone else's perspective, and these book recommendations will give your kids the incomparable gift of being able to "travel" the world through story.

Stephanie Langford, writer at EntreFamily.com

GIVE YOUR CHILD THE WORLD

Raising Globally Minded Kids
One Book at a Time

JAMIE C. MARTIN

ZONDERVAN

Give Your Child the World
Copyright © 2016 by Jamie C. Martin

Requests for information should be addressed to:
Zondervan, 3900 *Sparks Dr. SE, Grand Rapids, Michigan 49546*

ISBN 978-0-310-34414-8 (ebook)

Library of Congress Cataloging-in-Publication Data

Names: Martin, Jamie C., author.
Title: Give your child the world : raising globally minded kids one book at a time / Jamie C. Martin.
Description: Grand Rapids : Zondervan, 2016. | Includes bibliographical references and index.
Identifiers: LCCN 2016004192 | ISBN 9780310344131 (softcover)
Subjects: LCSH: Child rearing--Religious aspects--Christianity. |
 Parenting--Religious aspects--Christianity. | Children--Books and reading. | Teenagers--Books
    and reading. | Children's literature--History and criticism. | Young adult literature--History and
    criticism.
Classification: LCC BV4529 .M36235 2016 | DDC 248.8/45--dc23 LC record available at http://lccn.
    loc.gov/2016004192

Published in association with Jenni Burke of D. C. Jacobson & Associates LLC, an Author
Management Company www.dcjacobson.com

Cover design: connie gabbert | design + illustration
Cover illustration: © Iveta Angelova / © natashanast / Shutterstock®
Interior design: Kait Lamphere

First printing April 2016 / Printed in the United States of America

To the children of Newtown, Connecticut,
a place that has given our family so much

CONTENTS

FOREWORD

I was thrilled when I first saw those two pink lines on our debut pregnancy test. We were going to be parents! The two of us, ever the global wanderers, were going to do the grown-up thing and settle down as a family of three.

As those nine months crawled by and my belly stretched, friends and family frequently reminded us of the well-known advice to sleep while we could because we wouldn't be able to in just a few months. We knew that; we did. But during all those weeks of setting up a crib and stocking our diaper stash, I wrestled with an even heftier thought: once we became parents, we'd no longer travel as we used to.

You see, my husband, Kyle, and I met overseas, in Kosovo, and we continued to gallivant around the world in the early days of our relationship. We knew that once we had kids, we wouldn't be able to toss on a backpack, catch a cab to the airport, and buy tickets for whatever flight was next. We subscribed to the commonly held belief that children shrink the parameters of the world to the confines of the local butcher, baker, and big-box retail store.

I'm happy to report that almost a decade later, the opposite has proven true. Our three kids don't slow us down from the joy of hopping on planes, trains, and automobiles; in fact, they expand our world to horizons I never thought possible. Their vagabond hearts win over countless cultures, giving us entrance to new relationships and otherworldly experiences.

But the truth is, as much as our clan loves to leave our front door and travel, most of our days *are* spent on the couch in our living room and on the grass in our own backyard. Library trips, grocery runs, and karate practice are much more likely to be a part of our days than a trip to Zambia—love that journey as we may.

Books are the answer to our wanderlust. From the moment we crack open the cover, a book transports us to worlds exotic and unknown. We breathe in the glory of different colors, landscapes, and cultural mores. Books are like passports—but so much cheaper to use!

Jamie's wisdom within these pages captures the beauty of what happens when books and a love of the world meet. This side of eternity, there are few greater love stories. And the incredible thing? We can introduce our kids to this love affair right at our dining room tables, pages splayed with pigment and tale. Along with us, our kids can smell the smells of the Middle East and touch the textures of South America. Their hearts can melt for God's greatest creation: people. Diverse, beautiful people.

I'm thankful Jamie has written this book, because when our adventurous family is unable to drive our minivan to the airport, we can do the next best thing—walk over to the bookshelf, choose one of the many books she suggests, and snuggle in together on the couch. Destinations: uncharted. Compasses: ready.

Tsh Oxenreider, theartofsimple.net

THE WORLD IN OUR HOMES

I woke up this morning and got out of bed.
My sheets were made in Vietnam.

I took a shower and dressed.
My shirt was made in Indonesia.

I made the children oatmeal with raisins.
The raisins had been grown in California.

I watched my son ride his bike outside.
His bike was made in China.

We came inside and read a fairy tale.
The story took place in Germany.

I brought out blocks for the kids to build with.
They were handcrafted in the U.S.

While the children played, I put on some music.
We listened to a collection of African folk songs.

During the kids' rest time, I worked on this book.
My computer was made in China.

In the afternoon we watched a documentary.
It transported us to Japan.

I called my husband to see if he could bring home dinner.
He ordered takeout from our favorite Mexican restaurant.

We sat down to eat as a family.
Our dishes were made in Thailand.

After the children went to bed, Steve and I watched a movie.
It took place in England.

Then I brushed my teeth and tiredly crawled into bed.
My sheets were made in Vietnam.

*Could it be we're already more connected
to the world than we realize?*

PART ONE

FALLING IN LOVE WITH THE WORLD

The Martin Family: Jonathan, Steve, Elijah, Jamie, Trishna

CHAPTER 1

THE GOOD EARTH: A LOVE STORY

In the beginning God created the heavens and the earth . . . Then God
looked over all he had made, and he saw that it was very good!
Genesis 1:1, 31 NLT

I sat by the edge of the island, watching God show off. If you've ever had the chance to visit Hawaii, you know that's what he likes to do there.

Miraculously, I had the beach all to myself as a full moon crept over the horizon and the crimson violet of sunset shadowed nearby palm trees. To my right stood the turquoise guesthouse where we were staying, to my left the turquoise waves of the Pacific Ocean. The kids had left behind the remains of their day's work: inflatable inner tubes piled lopsided in a corner, crumbling sandcastles with plastic shovels nearby. With jet lag as their bedtime companions, they'd headed eagerly inside for an early sleep.

I didn't try to hold back my tears as I whispered lavish thanks to heaven for this idyllic vacation. But Hawaii wasn't our final destination. In less than one week we'd board new flights and land in the Philippines, where we'd spend the summer as part of my husband's job with Love146, a charity working to abolish child trafficking and exploitation.

In less than one week, we'd drive by hundreds of cardboard shacks—and those who dwell in them—on our way to Love146's safehome, where a dozen girls live, girls who have suffered some of the worst atrocities known to mankind. Resting on the sand surrounded by nature's splendor, how could I reconcile these two extremes? Hawaiian sunsets on one hand, child slavery on the other?

My own kids taught me how that summer. No matter where we went, they were all there. *Present.* My ten-year-old daughter, Trishna, laughing in the ocean or giggling with trafficking survivors her own age. My nine-year-old son,

Jonathan, snorkeling alongside colorful fish or going with Daddy to buy Legos for Filipino boys who'd never had any. My youngest, eight-year-old Elijah, digging with a mission in the sand or gazing with empathic eyes at the signs of extreme poverty on the streets.

Children don't let the darkness of world overshadow its beauty. They don't make judgments. They just try to love—whatever and whoever stands in front of them.

You've seen this in your own kids, who live with awe and wonder as their daily companions—picking up a rock to examine, planting a spontaneous kiss on your cheek, staring at a hawk overhead, beaming a sudden smile at a stranger. And you know what? Almost always, the stranger smiles back. For a split second, our little one's unconditional love brightens someone's world.

Children start out this way, but often something happens. We recognize it because it most likely happened to us too. Worries crowd out wonder. Selfishness crowds out sacrifice. Longing for more crowds out love for what is. Problems crowd out people. Knowing this, how can we strengthen our kids' natural love for the world so it sticks around for the long haul? How can we grow it into their lifelong companion, one that leads them to care for others because of their deep passion for this planet and the people on it?

Thankfully, we have at our fingertips a miracle vaccine—one that can boost our children's immunity to the world's distractions and heaviness. *Story.* Well-chosen stories connect us with others, even those on the other side of our globe. Build your kids' lives on a story-solid foundation and you'll give them armor to shield themselves from the world's cynicism. You'll give them confidence to persevere in the face of life's conflicts. You'll give them a reservoir of compassion that spills over into a lifetime of love in action.

This is what happens when you combine falling in love with the world *and* falling in love with story. The world changes, one heartbeat at a time. Here's how it happened for me.

HOW I FELL IN LOVE WITH THE WORLD

Since I wrote a book about reading your way around the world, you might imagine I was raised in a jet-setting family that traveled regularly to Earth's far corners. But you wouldn't even be close.

I grew up in Wilmington, North Carolina, not in a traveling family or a wealthy one. I remember exactly one childhood vacation—a road trip to neighboring Tennessee on a visit to relatives.

Though I wasn't raised with riches, my life overflowed with blessings. The two most important were the people who encouraged me to develop a relationship with books and the world: Mom and Dad.

I inherited my curious soul from my father. On the weekends, we drummed up adventure—the local (and cheap!) kind. Our search often took us to the cinema, where for the price of a movie ticket we journeyed somewhere new. Other days we took to the road in his sputtering Toyota Celica. After picking a destination and saying a prayer that the car would make it there, we drove a couple of hours in our chosen direction. After our arrival, we explored, grabbed a bite to eat, and headed home again. We visited old ruins, new shopping malls, battlefields, and hole-in-the-wall diners. By the time I hit my teen years, my heart for travel beat strong—and it had never even taken a trip out of the country.

While Dad nurtured my love for adventure, Mom encouraged my interest in books. In the midst of the busy schedules and routine challenges of family life, she drove me to the library every third Monday for years. The hallway to the upstairs children's section—with its stacks of yet-unread inspiration and even a computer in the 1980s—was the entrance to my childhood Narnia. Magic lay on those shelves. Without any money I had access to everything . . . and everywhere. I grew up spending hours on my bed, head propped in my hands, venturing west in a covered wagon with Laura Ingalls, to the shores of Prince Edward Island with Anne Shirley, and in a twister with Dorothy straight to Oz.

As a young teenager, my love for other cultures, lands, and people evolved into a deep passion. All those voyages around the world between the covers of a book had kindled my empathy and grown my compassion. My hours of reading had convinced me that people were people, no matter where they lived. At the core, all of us shared a common connection. Although I'd never been on an airplane, I decided I wanted to be a missionary overseas, serving and devoting my life to those in need. My high school friends remember well that I even took to spinning a globe when we hung out together, closing my eyes, and landing my finger on a random country. When I opened them, I'd laugh and announce, "My husband is going to be from _____."

WHERE THE SPINNING GLOBE REALLY LANDED

At the age of sixteen, I had an opportunity to take a six-week summer mission trip to Eastern Europe. Feeling both excited and nervous about the idea, I wanted confirmation that it was the right experience and the right time. I sat cross-legged on the sofa with a navy-blue leather-covered Bible in my lap, asking for divine guidance. Suddenly I felt a startling whisper speak to my soul: "You will meet the person you're going to marry there."

"Excuse me, *what?*" Not wanting to be embarrassed or teased, I told no one. I filed the message away in my heart—alongside plenty of other hormone-induced wishful thinking.

I said yes to the trip (as if any other answer would be possible after a message like that!). And believe me, when I first arrived, I spent plenty of time considering which guy might be The One. But then something incredible happened, something highly unlike my type-A-perfectionist teen self. In the busy rush of travel and adventure that summer, I forgot all about the message spoken to my spirit.

Then another wildly wondrous event occurred.

I fell in love.

Steve had joined the trip from his home in England. By the end of those six weeks, I couldn't imagine life without him. The day we left to go back to our respective countries, my heart broke. This being pre-internet days, there was no email—no easy way to stay in touch. Phone calls to England cost two dollars a minute, and sixteen-year-olds without jobs didn't have that kind of money (though, much to Dad's dismay, we ran up some pretty high bills anyway). With a wide ocean separating us, we had no clue when—or if—we would ever see each other again.

Six years later, I stood outside a Southern church in the humid, post-thunderstorm summer air. Dad waited beside me as we listened for our cue in the music. At just the right beat in Pachelbel's "Canon in D," the heavy mahogany doors flew open, and we began our walk. Stepping forward in a surreal bridal daze, I smiled and looked down the aisle at the young man standing there: Steve, my best friend and soulmate. Turns out I wasn't crazy when God delivered that message years before. He had done the impossible—crossing obstacles, mistakes, and even oceans to get us to that moment.

But the global story of my life was only just beginning.

BUILDING A GLOBAL FAMILY

As typically happens, a handful of years into our marriage, we started to think about a family. We decided that if we couldn't have biological children, we would consider adoption. Yet just a few months later we found out I was pregnant, and soon a baby boy joined our family. Jonathan's name means "God's gift," and he has lived up to that name in many ways, both expected and unexpected. I expected crying, sleepless nights, and around-the-clock feedings. I didn't expect that this little one had arrived to give us a passion for children around the world.

Caring for a baby was *harder* than I had ever thought possible. Needy in every way, Jonathan depended on us for everything. I'm with Anne Lamott, who declared in her bestseller *Bird by Bird*, "having a baby is like suddenly getting the world's worst roommate."[1] Didn't everyone know that I had no clue what I was doing, yet I had been entrusted with a life? At the same time, a feeling kept rushing over me that I couldn't quite shake: Steve and I had a mature, stable marriage, yet this baby transition was rocking us to our core. It required all we had, and then some, stretching us way beyond what we had imagined. Though we had prepared as much as we could have, we still found it difficult to meet our child's constant needs. What about all the children who didn't have someone to do for them what we were doing for our son? Maybe more children needed what our family had to offer. Should we consider adopting?

Steve and I searched the Bible for direction. Verses like James 1:27, which we had read hundreds of times, now took on new meaning:

> Religion that God our Father accepts as pure and faultless is this: to look after orphans and widows in their distress and to keep oneself from being polluted by the world.

Suddenly adoption seemed to be everywhere. I'd turn on the television and see Oprah talking about it. I'd open the mail to find a magazine article about it. A friend showed up out of the blue on our doorstep with a book about it. By this time we believed there was a child for us somewhere in the world, but where?

An online search made my head spin. Talk about too much information! Countries to choose from, mountains of paperwork to complete, plenty of hefty fees to pay (and did I mention we didn't have the money to pay them?).

But Steve and I had learned through our cross-cultural love story that if God has a plan, he can overcome any challenges. So when "overwhelm" would strike, I would shut down my computer, take a deep breath, and utter a simple prayer: "Jesus, if this is really the next step for our family, make it happen. You create a connection. You lead us to our child." We decided to wait for clarity. We wouldn't take another step until we knew for sure we were on the right path.

It didn't take long.

By this point in our married life, Steve and I had taken positions with the global charity Mercy Ships, an organization that uses hospital ships to offer free medical care in poverty-stricken areas. When Jonathan was a few months old, our boss asked Steve to fly to Liberia, West Africa, in his role as a videographer to film stories and surgeries on board one of the ships. My heart leapt at the news—could this assignment guide us to our next child? Sure enough, a few days into his trip Steve visited an orphanage that had completed the legal process necessary to do adoptions to the States. Feeling the confirmation and peace we'd been waiting for, we began to climb the necessary mountains of paperwork, one page at a time. After several months, we did what all soon-to-be adoptive families do eventually: we began to wait . . . for the phone call that would change everything.

Just when I thought I couldn't handle the wait any longer, the call came. It came on a sweltering afternoon in late summer. I held the phone in trembling hands, mind spinning, as I listened to the person on the other end tell me about the newest member of our family, six-month-old Elijah.

Babies often arrive with unforeseen challenges like colic or ear infections. Yet when I brought our newest addition home, he was at death's door, sick with malaria and parasites. I carried him off the airplane and introduced him to his daddy, who drove us straight to the pediatrician. The emergency room at the nearest children's hospital soon followed. Some moments in the weeks ahead found us wondering if he would make it, if we'd ever get the chance to know and love this boy. With wild thanks to the medical care he received during his first few weeks in the United States, Elijah has been healthy ever since then. Steve and I certainly had our hands full in the months that followed, plenty to keep us busy, out of trouble, and a bit overwhelmed as we cared for two baby boys. And yet our family wasn't quite complete after his arrival. Something, or I should say *someone*, was still missing.

PREPARING OUR HEARTS FOR A MIRACLE

An ancient Chinese legend states that an invisible red thread connects those who are meant to be part of each other's lives. The thread may tangle or stretch, but it will never break. About a year after Elijah settled into our family, we started to feel a tug, a pulling, on our spirits. That tug led us all the way to India.

India, a country of great beauty and great need, had been on our hearts for some time. So when our thoughts turned toward adoption once more, sensing another child might be out there for us, we began to research the country's international adoption policies. And that's how we found Trishna. We first saw her on an adoption agency's list of "waiting children." This meant the children had been approved for adoption, but for some reason—age, health, or disability—had not yet found a family. This smiling girl with the tight black curls, the frilly pink dress, and the glasses had spent her first four years in an orphanage. She had developmental delays as well as a significant visual impairment. Her eye condition was degenerative—it would worsen with age, eventually leading to blindness.

Deep breaths, Jamie. The whole idea seemed crazy—we had two toddler boys! Motherhood had already stretched me to my limits. Yet the soul-tug continued. Steve and I took tentative steps forward, praying all the while that the door would shut if this wasn't wise.

The door stayed open.

The adoption agency sent us Trishna's massive file to review. An inch-thick stack of papers, most of them medical reports, sat intimidatingly on my desk. The officials wanted to make sure we understood her conditions completely. India has high-quality medical care, and Trishna had visited many doctors. In examining the file, I came across extensive eye diagrams, X-rays, and terminology way beyond my comprehension. Thankfully, we knew a top eye surgeon from our work with Mercy Ships. We sent him the paperwork to ask for his professional opinion. Maybe this little girl had been misdiagnosed; maybe she didn't have the severity of disease indicated.

But his report didn't come back hopeful. "This condition is easy to diagnose and she has all the symptoms of it," our friend emailed back.

More deep breaths, Jamie. I began asking God to prepare us to raise a child with a significant disability. I started researching her conditions online and learning Braille. One morning during this process, while going about my regular mommy routine, I reached toward a high shelf to put a book away when I felt an inner voice suddenly speak:

"Why aren't you praying for me to heal her?"

I closed the glass door of the bookcase and leaned my head against my hand in wonder and surprise. It was as if the red thread connecting me with our soon-to-be daughter had received a huge heave forward. I knew we were being led to Trishna, but I hadn't considered that we might be the audience to a miracle as well.

Several months later I sat with our daughter in the office of a highly respected eye surgeon near our home. The air got heavy and the room began to swirl as

I tried to process his words: "Trishna only has a minor visual impairment. Her condition is not degenerative."

I walked hand in hand with my new preschooler out to the car, bright sun reflecting off my tears as the reality of what had just happened sunk deep into my soul.

God had healed our daughter before we'd even met her.

GOODNESS IN THE IMPERFECTION

In case you've lost count, we have a total of four nationalities represented in our family of five. Looking back, I never imagined this mini–United Nations we've created. I didn't plan it this way, but by taking one small step at a time we ended up here.

Don't get me wrong—life in our diverse family is not glamorous. The minutiae of most mamas fill my days to overflow: endless laundry, dinners in progress, sibling conflicts, learning, growing, and making mistakes. It's the stuff of life in action: days of living on mission and days of living in mess. Both equally valuable for knitting our hearts together.

But in the middle of the imperfection and the challenges, when mama-overwhelm threatens to strike, I send the kids outside to play, sit down on the couch, and pick up a book. Story takes center stage and problems fade. I connect with characters who remind me of life's bigger picture. I walk beside them in their struggles, learning from their successes and failures. I'm reminded that I'm not alone. I fall in love with this good earth again.

Parents naturally get concerned when we look at the state of the globe today. And it's true—your children and mine will one day inherit a world filled with unique issues and problems. But this is no accident. They have been chosen to lead their generation through its difficulties. Destined for this moment in history. With love, faith, and compassion firmly rooted in their spirits thanks to the power of story, they'll be able to see the people beyond the headlines. Nothing will be too much for them. Our job is to fill their lives with that love, faith, and compassion today—so they can rest their feet on a story-solid foundation in their tomorrows. Let's get started.

CHAPTER 2

PRACTICAL WAYS TO INVITE THE WORLD INTO YOUR HOME

The wide world is all about you: you can fence yourselves in, but you cannot forever fence it out.

J. R. R. Tolkien, *The Fellowship of the Ring*

S teve and I had a small rented apartment, a tight budget, and a few pieces of hand-me-down furniture in our newly married days. But when I walked by the framed print of the Eiffel Tower at Target, I knew I had to buy it. That twenty-dollar purchase, which stretched our funds to the max, represented something. Our heart, our vision, our world. It brought back memories of global adventures. It brought back the sense of smallness I felt while standing underneath the towering Parisian metal structure, an edifice that existed long before we did and would remain long after. Sure, we might settle down for a while. But we could at least remember the world's bigger picture, keeping our own day-to-day problems in perspective by comparison. Hanging the frame on our sparse, white walls, I exhaled. Much better. Seventeen years, three children, and several houses later, I still pass it daily.

Of course, a lot has happened since then. Adding three children from three continents to our family in less than three years, for example, certainly brought me face-to-face with my own limitations—as a mom, a wife, and a person. At one point, we had a four-, three-, and two-year-old under our roof. Only dependence on God and grace for each imperfect moment allowed me to keep up with all that family life required of me.

When the dust settled, and as Jonathan, Elijah, and Trishna began to get older, questions started nagging me.

- How could I connect my family with this incredible world?
- How could I introduce my children to the countries that will be part of our lives forever?
- How could I inspire them to learn, to care, and to eventually influence?

I came to realize that bringing a global perspective into our homes doesn't have to be complicated or abstract. It can be downright practical.

SIMPLE IDEAS THAT MAKE A BIG DIFFERENCE

This book's primary focus is on quality children's literature that introduces the globe and its people to your kids. As you read and discover new places together, you'll naturally want to learn more. That's where this chapter comes in. Using the ideas that follow, you can nurture a larger vision in your family—transforming it into a place where it's just as common for your kids to think of the world beyond your borders as it is for them to ask what's for dinner. (And if you're like me, you get asked that a lot!)

Read through this list and choose a couple of suggestions that resonate with you and make sense for this season of your life. Don't feel as if you have to try all of them at once. Starting simple and staying inspired beats burning out and giving up any day. After you integrate a few of these tips into your life, you may want to try others as well. They will broaden your global perspective and give your kids an even bigger curiosity about the world—a curiosity that will lead you back to the bookshelves again!

Approach Home Décor with a Global Touch

Keep an eye out for worldwide inspiration as you decorate your home. One of the first purchases Steve and I made after we bought our first house was an antique map of the world. We paid to have it professionally matted and framed, and we hung it above our living room fireplace. Its front-and-center location helped to keep our focus on the global dreams we shared and the impact we hoped to one day have on the world.

Place maps and globes in prominent places—areas where you and your children can easily access and consult them. You can find maps that fill an entire wall or are small enough to lie flat on the kitchen counter. Choose whatever appeals to you and works best in the space you have available. We have another world map hanging in our dining room, a third upstairs in the hallway, as well as a globe and a U.S. map downstairs at kid level.

If you are a missionary or military family or simply have moved now and then, consider displaying something from each place you've lived. Before we had children, Steve and I moved six times in seven years of marriage. We bought a watercolor print of each place we had lived—England, Washington D.C., North Carolina. We put them in inexpensive frames and placed them in the hallway. This is a great way to remember how far you've come as a family and the places you've loved along the way. You can do the same with spots where you've vacationed—or even places that you'd love to go someday, creating a dream or prayer wall. Invite your kids to fall more deeply in love with the world by placing objects in your home that remind them of it each day.

Introduce Foods with an International Flair

Introducing my children to ethnic foods at a young age has provided our family many inexpensive foreign experiences right here at home. Most supermarkets have an international aisle these days, which makes it simple to try a new food at the beginning of each month or whenever you shop.

Start with sweet tastes if your kids are not yet adventurous eaters—make this an exciting experiment, not a battleground. Don't force the issue if no one shows interest, but set the example yourself. Do the same if you live in an area with ethnic restaurants. Instead of always dining at the same spots, branch out every once in a while to try something new—consider it a field trip for the whole family.

Now That You Have Those Maps and Globes—Use Them!

When your kids sample cuisine from another area of the world, don't just let them eat it and leave the table. Take an extra minute, before or after the meal, to locate where your dinner originated. Do the same when a country arises in conversation—via a news report, a question your child asks, or a friend far away you're about to pray for. This small step goes miles in acquainting our little ones with the world in their elementary years. When we're at the table, I will often grab our globe and point to the location we're discussing, then walk around to show it to each child.

Google Earth currently fascinates our kids. If you have a computer handy when other countries come up in your family's conversations, travel to those places via Google at no cost. How incredible that we can browse the streets and lanes on the other side of the earth without ever leaving home. (Steve and the kids actually ended up behind the Google car one day, and they're currently frozen in the frame of one of our former neighborhoods in Connecticut!)

But don't feel as though you have to reach for a globe or map every day. Do it when you're inspired, and let go of any guilt when you're not. Simply having an intention to highlight the world to your kids makes a difference.

Explore a New Country Each Month

Why not study a new country on a regular basis? Our family does this through Little Passports, a subscription service that organizes it for you. The first month we joined, a small suitcase arrived containing a passport, wall map, activity stickers, and other introductory information. Each subsequent month a packet of information arrives about another country—with a boarding pass, souvenirs, activity sheet, photos, and a stamp/sticker to add to your "little passport." You also get access to online games about the location. So far we've "traveled" to Brazil, Japan, France, Australia, and many other destinations. The kids love it, and I've enjoyed it as much as they have. Find out more at http://www.littlepassports.com/.

Of course you can adapt the same idea and put it together yourself. With the internet's magic, it wouldn't take long to compile, create, and download an international adventure of your own—complete with photos, games, and recipes to try out. This fun exploration helps young children begin to grasp the different ways people around the globe live.

Celebrate an Annual Heritage Day

Each year our family celebrates India Day, Liberia Day, America Day, and England Day. India Day and Liberia Day occur on the anniversary of the days that we first met Trishna and Elijah. America Day is on Jonathan's half-birthday, and England Day is on Steve's birthday every year. We hang a large flag of the chosen country, play cultural music, decorate the table, and make or buy a traditional meal for dinner. Trishna and Elijah also have clothes from their birth countries they like to wear. After the initial year of celebrating heritage days in our house (which required ordering the flags, music, and décor), we found that there is little preparation required to have a great celebration.

You can adopt this custom whether or not you have family members from other parts of the world. Do you have a specific heritage in your family tree you want to acknowledge? A country your family is connected to somehow? Is there a place you dream of going to someday? Celebrating an annual heritage day is a simple tradition your family will enjoy and remember.

Pay Attention to the News (but Not Too Much Attention)

The news surrounds us in this 24/7, ever-connected culture, and much of it depresses instead of encourages. Exposing our young kids to current headlines isn't the most effective way to facilitate their love for the world. Before the age of nine, children occupy an inner realm where it's difficult to completely distinguish between fantasy and reality. Surround them with the good things about our planet during this precious period of their lives. If your family is passionate about a specific cause or issue, don't focus on its complexities or darkness when your children are young. Instead talk about the role your family plays and how it helps. This empowers kids and fills them with the belief that they can make a difference.

Now that our three children are all over age ten, we discuss current events more often than before—usually around the dinner table. They don't read the news themselves yet, but as parents, Steve and I filter in what seems appropriate. Older tweens and teens will naturally want to interact with the headlines on their own, so find a source you trust and feel they can handle. I like *Youngzine* (http://www.youngzine.org/) as a starting point, an online news magazine for children. And for middle or high schoolers, check out *CNN Student News* (http://www.cnn.com/studentnews). The amount of news in a family's life will vary widely. Whatever your level of exposure, use it as an opportunity to help your children understand the world they live in.

Make Family Dinners a Priority

A regular dinnertime creates strong bonds, but you can't bond if you're not there. Now, I know what you're thinking, moms and dads of little people. You know how it goes at this time of day: everyone is exhausted, the kids start to bicker, you start to lose it, and soon you glance at your spouse across the table (only a glance, mind you, because forget any decent conversation) with eyebrows raised, thinking, "What have we done?"

I get it. Steve and I have exchanged many such desperate looks over the years. When we had a four-, three-, and two-year-old, we fed them first and ate together as a couple after they had gone to bed. Seasons of survival mode come to every family, so never feel guilty for doing what it takes to make it through them. But hold tightly to your ideals as well. Statistics show that kids who grow up having four or more dinners with their family each week are less likely to do drugs, consider suicide, or develop an eating disorder.[2] They are also far more likely to absorb the culture, heartbeat, and faith of your family.

My home finally has less chaos around our dinner table and more quality— interesting questions asked, more attention paid to the answers shared, inspiration dispensed as we talk about the details of our day's work. The moments aren't perfect, but they are *ours*. And that's what matters most.

Answer Their "Why-Why-Why" Questions—Sometimes

Young kids ask tons of questions. If you think about it, you'll see how this shows their enthusiasm for life and their eagerness to learn—the very qualities we want to encourage! But these constant queries often come at inopportune moments—like when you've picked up the phone for an important call, or when you've been peppered with similar questions all day, or when you finally decide you must get a minute of quiet or you'll burst.

Here's what I do: when I have paper and pen nearby, I'll jot their question down (if I don't already know the answer) to research later. Or if I have a free moment and my laptop handy, I will satisfy their curiosity right then and there.

I used to feel guilty if I didn't do this as soon as one of my kids asked a question. I thought I might miss a fabulous learning opportunity by not responding to them immediately. But just because our modern-day technology allows us to answer our children's questions in one minute or less, it doesn't mean we always *should*. Doing so encourages both instant gratification and an excessive dependence on screens, neither of which are habits we want for our little ones. Sometimes it's okay to hold a question in your mind, to wonder and wrestle with it—it's more than okay, it's beneficial for developing critical and creative-thinking skills.

Let your kids fall in love with this fascinating world by helping them discover how it works—yet at the same time, don't feel compelled to do so all day, every day.

What Inspires You? Share It.

In his role as CEO of Love146, my husband works to abolish child trafficking and exploitation. His days overflow with dark stories of need and bright glimmers of hope and restoration, and he talks about the latter with our kids when he comes home. When we're inspired, we share it—because inspiration is contagious.

But you don't need a global job to offer your kids a love of other cultures. Simply share the parts of the world that interest you. It doesn't have to be overseas—it could be across the state or across the street. Have you traveled somewhere you loved? Get the photos out and show them. Is there a specific country that fascinates you? Talk about it. You may not get much enthusiasm back initially, but if you make this a habit, eventually your kids will join in. Inspiration leads to action, to curiosity, to learning. Don't overcomplicate the process; just let your own passion shine through your everyday life—let it naturally influence your home.

Sponsor a Child and Make the Globe Personal

The vast needs of our planet can feel overwhelming and abstract—even to adults. Since young children don't understand abstract concepts, we must find a practical way to bring the world to life. Kids *do* understand and identify with other kids, so sponsoring a child can be a perfect first step. Many reputable organizations like World Vision and Compassion International have in-depth sponsorship programs. Your monthly fee lifts a child out of poverty and offers him or her an education. In many cases you can interact with your sponsored child as a pen pal too—exchanging letters, photos, and even sending emails.

If you're deeply involved with a ministry or cause, your kids will also form a personal connection with the globe. During our summer in the Philippines in 2013, Jonathan, Elijah, and Trishna saw poverty up close in ways they never had experienced before. They also watched as our family followed God's call to respond. Even after our return, part of our hearts stayed behind. When the super typhoon Yolanda hit the Philippine shores later the same year, the kids remembered the people we knew there. They wanted to pray, help, and give. When we make the world personal for our children, we make it easier for them to love it.

Invite Globally Minded Friends into Your Lives

When I was an impressionable teen, my family invited Debbie, a young missionary passing through town, to stay with us for a few days. As I listened to her speak about her faith, her calling, and her travels, inspiration ignited inside me. When Debbie left, she agreed to write, and through our letters that year she encouraged me to point my life in a faith-filled, meaningful direction. Who knew that a short stay in someone's home could have so much influence?

Keep an eye out for ways to welcome friends with a global perspective into your home—it could be an exchange student, a refugee in your town, an aid worker passing through, or a neighbor with a different background. Through reaching out to others, we nurture and deepen relationships, informally introduce our children to another place, and get a glimpse of what God is doing around the world. This takes us one step closer to developing a global focus and may even become, like it did in my case, a life-changing connection.

Start a Positivity Bean Jar

Bean jars sit on the shelves of many elementary school classrooms. When a student or the entire class makes a good choice or succeeds in some way, one or more dry beans get added to the empty container. After the level finally reaches the top, the children earn a reward.

I liked the idea of bringing this concept into our home, but I felt a little uncomfortable about the reward aspect. I aspire to teach my kids that good is its own reward. What if our right choices benefitted *others*, instead of ourselves?

So we started a positivity bean jar. Each time I see kindness, sharing, generosity, or compassion modeled in our home, in goes one or more beans. I also put them in for words spelled correctly, math facts learned, and other skills attempted and conquered. Each bean equals ten cents and when the level reaches the top, we dump them out, count them, and the children donate the money to the charity of their choice. Read more about our jar by searching my blog, http://www.steadymom.com, for "positivity jar."

Learn More about Ethical Spending

Does it ever feel as if any effort you make only adds a drop to the massive bucket of global need? I wrestle with that feeling too. But when we understand that in this connected world of ours nearly every dollar spent impacts someone on the other side of it, we see how much influence we hold. When we change our spending, we change others' lives. If we want justice on earth—to see those who work paid for their efforts, to watch slavery come to an end worldwide—then our purchasing dollars matter.

Learning about ethical spending for the first time can be overwhelming, but thankfully *The Better World Shopping Guide* by Ellis Jones simplifies the process. The book grades companies based on different factors—including environmental stewardship and human rights—then rates them with a letter grade, A through F. I carried this small guide in my purse for years as I slowly discovered which companies to support at the grocery store, the mall, and online.

Tsh Oxenreider, who wrote this book's foreword and blogs at *The Art of Simple*, has also compiled an ethical shopping guide online. You can find it at http://theartofsimple.net/shopping.

One word of caution from personal experience: Don't give in to guilt when it comes to your spending. At times I've felt almost paralyzed to act if something I needed to buy wasn't from a great company and I lacked either the funds or the time to make a better choice. In the words of Theodore Roosevelt: "Do what you can, with what you have, where you are." It won't be perfect, but it will be *something*. Like a friend told me, "Even if all I'm able to do in my current situation and income is avoid F companies most of the time, at least I'm trying."

Turn Your Travels, Near or Far, into a Learning Opportunity

The rest of our family was already in the packed car, waiting to leave on our road trip south, when Jonathan bounded down the front-porch steps. He held several pieces of taped-together paper, which waved like a kite tail as he eagerly ran our way. Quickly he explained that he had used the printer to make copies of the eastern half of our large U.S. map—the areas we would pass through on our trip. More tape in hand, he secured his home-crafted map to the dashboard.

"This way we can track our route through different states." I smiled a mama's encouragement his way and thanked him for the good idea.

As well as using maps to navigate and track our journeys, we also have a tradition of buying travel journals for our kids when we explore a new place. Every day or so, we'll get them out in a quiet moment and chronicle our recent adventures. For my reluctant writers, I offer to write the entry as they dictate it—after all, this is not an exercise in handwriting but memory making. I love the journals from Gadanke, which include a variety of prompts to get ideas flowing, but you can also use a blank journal and make up your own starter questions—what we did today, what we saw, and what we ate. (My kids always love answering the latter!)

Place a Prayer Bowl in the Center of Your Table

Create a daily ritual that reminds your family to think of others around the world. Place a bowl or jar in the center of the dining table and on small pieces of paper write the names of countries, people, or issues—whatever tugs at your heart globally. Fold the papers in half and place them in the bowl. Before you bless your food and eat, or afterward if that works better for hungry little ones, have one family member choose a slip of paper and say a quick prayer. Rotate around the table so that each mealtime someone new has the chance to participate. This tradition allows everyone to take part—from the oldest to the youngest.

Not sure what or who to pray for? Simple is always better. Make it personal by including relatives who live at a distance and issues in your own neighborhood.

Open a Book and Travel the World—Together

One of the simplest and most rewarding ways we have found to learn about other people and countries is to read. And that brings me to the heart of this book. With nothing more than a library card, you are ready to foster a lifelong love of the world in your family.

Let's look now at how, and why, story is such a compelling way to give our children the world.

CHAPTER 3

THE POWER OF STORY

A sense of permanent worthwhileness surrounds really great literature.
Laughter, pain, hunger, satisfaction, love, and joy—the ingredients
of human life are found in depth and leave a residue of mental and
spiritual richness in the reader.
Gladys Hunt, *Honey for a Child's Heart*

I pick up our latest title and sit down in my favorite gray chair at the dining table. Noisy spirits, sibling squabbles, and daily distractions disappear as fiction transports us to another place and time. Whether we're reading about the enchanted wardrobe of Narnia or the blizzard-threatened prairies of Minnesota, the power of story plants us directly in the middle of the action. As the characters' struggles become our own, we root for good to win, and we grasp more deeply the story we are writing with our own lives.

But where do we start? Not all stories are created equal. This fact, combined with the sheer quantity of titles out there, can overwhelm parents searching for greatness to line their shelves. I've read hundreds of books to my children throughout their young lives and have spent hours looking for books for our own personal library. During that time one question has guided my efforts: *How can I choose the best for my family?* Once I knew what to look for, it became easier to put every book through the same filter. Here are the components I've found that make up an inspiring tale:

A Powerful Story Reflects Real-Life Struggles of Right and Wrong

"I've noticed something," Trishna mentioned one day as we drove around town on a mommy-daughter date. "Most stories have a good character and a bad one or something good that happens and something bad that comes after."

"That's so true," I answered, thrilled that she'd made this connection and was giving it serious thought. "It's because really, in life, there's only one story: the story of right and wrong, of good versus evil, of challenge and overcoming it."

We chatted about how boring it would be if a book's protagonist never had any difficulties. It wouldn't reflect real life. We learn from struggles and imperfections. That's why we're not looking for characters without any flaws. We know from history and family life that everyone has weaknesses, and the books we read should reflect this fact. We can learn from the choices, right *or* wrong, that characters make along the way.

Keep in mind, though, that for young children the best books have a clear distinction between good and bad. As readers get older—I'd say around age eight—they can handle more nuance and subtlety, including the idea that people aren't *all* good or *all* bad but usually a mix of both. Until then, stick with stories in which the contrast is evident.

A Powerful Story Helps Us Develop Compassion

I climbed the stairs, hoping to help a troubled boy find calm again. With a quick inner prayer for patience, I rubbed my son's back while discussing the argument that had just occurred with his brother, what had happened and why it was wrong to treat people that way, and what might be better next time.

As I stood up to leave the room, he said, "It's like the golden rule." We had just read a book about it that morning (*The Golden Rule* by Ilene Cooper). Once again I found myself thankful for a story's influence, growing our compassion and adding meaning to our everyday moments.

The books on the lists that follow will help your family grasp on a new level that what we have in common with our worldwide neighbors far outweighs what separates us. As children make that connection, it naturally develops compassion for their brothers and sisters around the globe and around the corner—because we all have similar needs, hopes, and desires. Great stories build an empathic foundation that leads to a life of service and concern for others.

A Powerful Story Inspires and Grows Our Character

"And thank you, God, that my boys are like Captain von Trapp, having the courage to stand up for what's right no matter what others do."

I uttered the words in the boys' bedroom at night after we'd finished watching *The Sound of Music*. Jonathan and Elijah flashed sleepy smiles my way as I finished the prayer. They'd recently begun studying World War II, so the deeper nuances of the film (beyond the incredible songs) touched and inspired them. They went to bed imagining their own inner hero.

We all have one, you know. And a powerful story (on the page or screen) quickens that hero's heartbeat within us. Well-chosen words touch and transform our souls—making us want to be better than we are right now. Nagging lectures from Mom and Dad simply can't compare with the lessons of a story whose time has come.

Newbery medal–winning author Katherine Paterson said that "the books we read in childhood are a rehearsal for experiences later in life."[3] I love this analogy. Creating a family culture of books means our kids have the chance to live a thousand lives before leaving our home. Isn't that incredible? They can travel the world (and beyond), all the while safe within our four walls. They can feel the pain of a character's flaws and learn from their mistakes, without having to experience the actual consequences. Far from a way to escape reality, reading actually prepares our children for real life in a unique way.

A Powerful Story Deepens Our Understanding of Language

Reading exposes children to a depth of language and vocabulary that gives them a huge academic advantage. Research cited in *The Read-Aloud Handbook* by Jim Trelease states that the more printed materials in a child's home, the higher that child's skills in reading, writing, and even math.[4] Finding pleasure in words and their intricacies also prepares our kids to become more successful writers and public speakers. But beyond purely academic benefits, a fuller command of language adds to our enjoyment of life.

As you search for the best stories to share with those you love, a quick flip-through of a book's pages will show you what type of language the author uses. Look for style and vocabulary that is a little beyond what kids can read for themselves when you're choosing a read-aloud, and for language they can more or less master alone when you select titles for individual reading. And while you're on the lookout, make sure you know how to spot twaddle.

Dictionary.com defines *twaddle* as "a term used to describe trivial or foolish speech or writing; nonsense." Charlotte Mason, a nineteenth-century British teacher who revolutionized educational philosophy in her time, coined the word. She believed in putting the best stories in children's hands—the most inspiring words by the most gifted authors. These books formed the foundation of her curriculum—the building blocks of greatness, so to speak. She wrote: "Even for their earliest reading lessons, it is unnecessary to put twaddle into the hands of children. That children like feeble and tedious . . . story books, does not at all prove that these are wholesome food; they like lollipops but cannot live upon them."[5]

Think of twaddle as dumbed-down literature for children. Examples include most books based on kids' television shows, abridged versions of classics that simplify the language and strip the meaning, and titles that don't leave scope for a child's blossoming imagination. If the majority of a child's literacy journey overflows with depth and richness, their educational life will do the same. The opposite is sadly true as well.

So should we banish all signs of twaddle from our homes forevermore? In a pure twaddle-free world, perhaps kids would never read a Dora the Explorer paperback, touch an abridged version of *Pollyanna*, or look at a kids' Bible with cartoon illustrations. But my children have done all three! And it's fine, honestly. Keep your focus on what you can do as you choose books, but don't beat yourself up for what you can't control. You've probably discovered this already, but perfectionism and parenting don't mix. Set yourself free from impossible standards and read that Dora book with all your heart: "Swiper, no swiping!" Say it proud, mamas and papas.

Just remember the 80/20 principle. In the same way you try to feed your children healthy food the majority of the time, try to make their diet of reading material nourishing the majority of the time. Then don't sweat the rest. When we go to the library, my children pick out the books they want and enjoy. Because we've raised them mostly on the best, their choices are usually, but not always, high quality. I browse the shelves myself and add plenty of soul-building titles to our rather large stack. If the kids add a few "dessert" titles to the mix, so be it! Maybe we'll have moments when we need something light, sweet, and fluffy anyway.

TEN WAYS TO BUILD A STORY-SOLID FOUNDATION FOR YOUR FAMILY

Finally, I'd like to offer a list of ideas to help you make reading a natural part of your family's life. Feel free to adjust or delete according to what suits you and yours.

1. Use the Library in a Way That Works for You

Our family has been through different seasons when it comes to library usage, including one in which taking my children there just didn't work for me (because of their young ages). During that time I still used the library by going alone and choosing books for the kids. It became a special tradition, as they looked forward to the surprises in store upon my return. If you don't have library access, think about what you can substitute instead. A book exchange with friends? Electronic books that you can download through a service like Overdrive.com? Making a wish list of books for relatives when they ask what to buy for holidays? Stocking up at garage sales? Do your best using what's available to you in this moment.

2. Don't Feel Tied to Bedtime Reading

Rarely in my life have I enjoyed bedtime reading with my kids, a fact I tried to hide for ages because it felt like the parenting police might show up and take me away. In all honesty, though, by the time evening arrives after a long day, I lack the patience to enjoy stories with my children. (Haven't you ever found yourself skipping pages here and there to reach the end of a book? And has your little one ever called you out on it?)

Bedtime isn't the only acceptable reading time. I prefer mornings, when I have the most energy. Or you might try snack time with the kids around the table when they get home from school. For years now I've found our best time for reading aloud to be during a meal—when little mouths are busy chewing, giving me a captive audience. If you try and fail, don't assume that reading aloud won't work for you—just get creative with your timing.

3. Invite the Whole Family

I realized several years into reading stories to the kids that Steve missed out on most of them since he was at work all day. So we began a family reading time after dinner, while everyone was still at the table. (Keep in mind that we tried this only after the kids were around age eight and had the attention span to keep up with us.) Our most successful readings as a family have been short—no more than ten or fifteen minutes, even if that means stopping in the middle of a chapter. Better to leave them wanting more than to have everyone give a sigh of relief when you're done. For families with children under eight, reading a short Bible passage or story might work well at dinner. We love the *Jesus Storybook Bible* for littles.

4. Drop a Book If It Isn't Connecting with Everyone

At one point, we'd started reading the Narnia Series together, and we reached a title within it that just didn't connect with everyone. I pulled out all the stops—doing crazy voices for characters, making the readings shorter, and taking time to discuss what we were reading. But it wasn't much fun since not all of us were enjoying it. Family reading is about bonding, about deepening relationships. You need everyone "in" for it to work. So, I thanked that well-written book and returned it to the shelf for another season. I've found that when I'm willing to do that, we've gone on to an even better title next—a good exercise for me in letting go of control.

5. Talk about What You're Reading Personally

Our kids need to see that reading isn't only a child's activity. Or worse—something assigned to endure until you can move on to something "fun." Accomplish this easily by setting the example yourself. Keep your own books on a side table in the dining room or other high-traffic area, somewhere the children will naturally notice. Take a moment here and there to describe a suspenseful plot twist that captivated you, or read a short quote aloud that they might appreciate. No pressure to read from someone else's list of official classics. Begin with your own interests, whatever they may be.

6. Use Audio Books

For parents with work commutes, for lengthy road trips, and for the auditory learner when Mom's or Dad's voice starts to wear thin, audio books save the day. Download one for yourself when you're folding the laundry or making dinner, or find a collection for the kids to choose from during afternoon quiet times. Discover new titles at audible.com, librivox.org, and your local library. If you have a child with dyslexia or a visual impairment, you may qualify for a subscription to LearningAlly.org. Our family has found it invaluable!

7. Go with the Interruptions When You Can

At times I cannot even get through a paragraph of reading aloud without an interruption. A cup spill sends a child rushing to clean up, someone falls off their chair with a loud bang, or there are back-to-back questions about plot or vocabulary. It can make a well-intentioned parent throw in the towel. But don't give up! Young kids' interruptions may be merely logistical, but as children grow, their interruptions have more to offer—an insight someone noticed, a comparison to another book's character, a deep meaning-of-life question. Don't skip these, even though they slow the reading down! Indeed, one could argue that these interruptions are precisely why we read: to learn how to think, to have new ideas and observations. Find a method that works for you to handle these moments. I taught my kids to raise their hands when they have a comment or question and wait until I can pause to listen to them. It doesn't work flawlessly, but it helps.

8. Get Dramatic

I've been known to get a little crazy while reading. If a character leaps to her feet in a frenzy, I do the same—surprising my unsuspecting audience at the dining table. Reading aloud should be fun for parents too, right? So add in a bit of drama when you feel like it. Experiment with different voices and accents. Welcome a little silliness from time to time. We may find that those moments leave the best reading memories in our children's minds.

9. Take Turns Reading

Don't feel as though you have to do all the reading aloud yourself. As your kids begin reading confidently, add them to the process. Have each person read a verse during your Scripture reading, or one stanza from a poem, or a page or chapter of a story. Not only does this provide a natural setting for everyone to practice reading for an audience, it adds to the family bonding of reading together, leading to the feeling that "this is just what we do, part of who we are."

10. Don't Stop When the Kids Get Older

Our reading times have only become better as my children have gotten older. We now have more interesting discussions about the real world, its wonders and its challenges. We make deeper connections as books lead us to new levels of thought. You aren't just reading to your kids until they can read to themselves. You're creating a culture of words, meaning, and the power of story—one that will grow richer as the years pass. Enjoy it!

GOOD BOOKS MAKE GOOD NEIGHBORS

When you move to a new neighborhood, you meet and get to know those who live nearby. Some may remain casual acquaintances—waving hello as you pull out of the driveway or chatting from the porch about the weather. Some may visit now and then, staying for a cup of tea or coffee, but you lose touch if you move again. Other neighbors, if you're radically blessed, become lifelong friends. They pop over to drop off something and stay for an hour. Their kids and yours are the same ages and love to play together. They have a spare key in case of emergencies. If you ever have to move, you take these relationships with you— deep connections that continue no matter where you go.

Use this analogy for the books you invite into your home. Some titles come for a quick visit. You read them and "meh"—they're okay, but they haven't touched your family deeply. They don't belong on the shelves permanently, so you wave goodbye from the porch as they take their leave. You'll also discover books that you want to spend more time with. Some titles will even journey through life with you, just like a close neighbor or dear friend. Simply seeing them on the shelf will inspire you. You'll want to read them again and again because they teach you something new every time.

Each family's list of favorites will be unique to them—the beautiful creation of your own reading culture. More than once I've finished a well-respected title that appears on many recommended lists, only to think "huh?" It just didn't meet me where I was at. Yet for another family or person, or even at another time, it might be life-changing.

When it comes to the hundreds of books I've included in the upcoming chapters, prepare yourself for a similar experience. Some you'll check out from the library, read, enjoy, and return. With other titles, you might turn the final page and say, "What on earth was Jamie thinking?" And some you'll invite to live on your shelves because they've touched your heart, helping you fall deeper in love with the world and each other.

PART TWO

READ THE WORLD

CHAPTER 4

THE JOY OF OTHER LANDS: HOW TO USE THE READING LISTS

The children should have the joy of living in far lands, in other persons, in other times—a delightful double existence; and this joy they will find, for the most part, in their story-books.
Charlotte Mason, *Home Education*

Putting together the perfect book list is like creating an ideal restaurant menu—you want all the choices to be delicious, but you also know people will order according to their different tastes and inclinations. The best option, therefore, is a well-spread buffet, where hungry diners browse the offerings and take what looks appetizing.

That's what I've done in the book lists that follow—prepared a feast of ideas and recommendations for you to choose from. What appeals most to your family will depend on what places in the world you're drawn to. Maybe you'd like to learn more about the land your ancestors came from, or perhaps you're getting ready to travel soon. Maybe there's a specific spot on your dream list or you support an organization working overseas. However they best suit you, adapt these lists to your traveling tastes and have fun!

HOW THE BOOKS ARE CATEGORIZED

Each chapter represents a different continent or area of the world: Africa; Europe; Asia; Middle East; North America; Latin America; and Australia,

Oceania, and the Polar Regions. I also created a general multicultural chapter of books that don't refer to a specific location but still contain a global theme.

Within each chapter, I've organized the books first by age range: 4–6 years, 6–8, 8–10, and 10–12. Often the standard age range listed for picture books is 4–8 years, but anyone who has ever had a four-year-old and an eight-year-old knows there's a drastic difference between the two! The standard age for chapter books is 8–12 years, but I've categorized those more specifically as well.

My goal was to choose the age in which I believe a child would get the *most* out of the book's message. Please look at these as general guidelines only; use your own judgment to decide what suits your kids. Children, even of the same age, vary widely in how sensitive they are to mature themes. I suggest previewing a book quickly before offering it to your child if you have any concerns.

Which books should you read aloud and which books should you let your kids read alone? As I compiled these recommendations, I assumed that the books in the 4–6 age category as well as most of the 6–8 range would be read aloud. This will vary depending on when your child learns to read fluently, of course. If a book makes a good "early reader" for a child to tackle alone, I've tried to note that in the description. Likewise, I've assumed that many of the 8–10 and 10–12 age books will be read by children on their own.

But as I mentioned in the last chapter, don't stop reading to your kids even if they can read to themselves. Choose titles for reading aloud that appeal most to you. In some cases, I've noted titles in these older categories that I think lend themselves well to reading aloud, and I hope that will help.

Within each age range, I've organized books alphabetically, first by the country's (or in some cases the region's) name, then within each country alphabetically by title. This will assist you in quickly finding what you're looking for.

At the beginning of each chapter, I've listed all the countries included in it. In some cases, I've put a book in the chapter of the culture it most represents, even if that isn't where the story takes place. For example, *One Green Apple*, by Eve Bunting, is about a young refugee from the Middle East who now finds herself adjusting to life in America. I put it in the Middle East chapter since that is the culture we learn most about as we read. Geography and history also go hand in hand, and many of the titles take place within a specific time period. Consult the index for a list of books arranged according to the historical time in which they occur, so you can use these recommendations to study history as well.

HOW THE BOOKS WERE CHOSEN

As I researched over a thousand titles for these lists, I aimed for quality over quantity. I tried to select books that truly convey the culture in which they take place with both inspiration and depth. My goal has been to sift through the piles of books myself, saving you as much time as possible—time that you can spend reading!

I've tried to choose titles that have lasting power—meaning they have been around long enough to prove themselves within the market. The more recent releases that I've included have had a successful launch and received rave reviews. Here and there I've added books that are out of print but were too good to pass up. There's a good chance your library will have them. *Give Your Child the World* can't possibly contain every worthwhile book with a multicultural theme, but I've done my best on the lists that follow to include titles that embody the soul of a classic as defined by educational pioneers Oliver and Rachel DeMille: "A work worth studying over and over again, because the student learns more each time."[6] Parents know all too well how young kids get attached to a specific book and ask to read it over and over. My hope is that these reading lists will introduce new favorites that won't be too painful to read multiple times.

As I worked on the book recommendations, I tried to keep in mind these words from C. S. Lewis: "No book is really worth reading at the age of ten which is not equally (and often far more) worth reading at the age of fifty and beyond."[7] Children shouldn't be the only ones getting important messages out of these books. We should too.

Most of the titles in the book lists are fiction choices, but I've added a few notable nonfiction books as well. Some children naturally gravitate more toward nonfiction and "the real world," so as you browse the lists, keep in mind your own kids' personalities and preferences. Our local library has shelves of nonfiction books about individual countries, and we often check these out when the kids take an interest in a certain place. I suggest pairing books from my book lists with these more general overviews to deepen your family's global understanding. From nonfiction we grasp the facts of a place, but from story we grasp the *heart*. Both have their unique roles to play when it comes to falling in love with the world.

Nearly all of the picture books that appear here I have held with my own hands and read either to myself or to the kids. At first I attempted to do the same with the chapter books, but I soon realized *Give Your Child the World* would be a decade in the making if I took time to do so. Instead, I read excerpts and also relied heavily on professional reviews from those who make books their business: *Publisher's Weekly*, *School Library Journal*, *Booklist*, and similar sources.

ON MATTERS OF FAITH

I grew up nervous and slightly intimidated by those who believed anything other than what I did. Instead of reaching out in friendship, I sometimes avoided those who differed from me. Surely this is not what Jesus meant when he told us to "love your neighbor as yourself." How can we love if fear or anxiety holds us back? Thankfully, books provide the perfect stage to discuss important issues, like faith, within the context of our families—to talk about not only what we believe but what others believe as well. By doing so, our kids develop greater empathy and a heart for those God loves around the world.

On the other hand, each child and family will be ready for such a discussion at a different time. Certain titles on my book lists include aspects of the religious beliefs dominant in the countries they portray. After a book's description, I have notated if that title contains a religious perspective. As a parent and teacher, let your internal compass guide you in both the titles you choose and the conversations that arise as you read.

But enough talk about the forthcoming books, let's get to the lists themselves. I suggest flipping through the second part of this book now to get a feel for it—then you can take it from there. Get ready to discover new titles that bring joy to your family and give your child the world.

CHAPTER 5

CHILDREN JUST LIKE ME: MULTICULTURAL BOOKS

Glancing through this chapter gives me an immediate surge of joy—there's so much here to inspire your kids, from preschool to middle school, with a curiosity about this fascinating planet of ours. Several of these recommendations hold nostalgic appeal for our family. I remember well the hectic yet sweet mornings when three littles surrounded me on our brown sofa, a stack of these books by my side.

Reading together didn't always go smoothly, mind you. There was the constant wiggling, the arguing over who gets to sit in Mommy's lap. Yet there was also the laughter, the occasional "Please, Mommy, just one extra story!" We got to know one another and the world a bit more every day with these titles as our companions. I know you will too!

MULTICULTURAL BOOKS FOR AGES 4–6

All the Colors of the Earth | Sheila Hamanaka

This book is a tribute to the shades of the earth—and the many children who live on it. The author compares each child's skin color to a beautiful part of nature— like "the whispering golds of late summer grasses." Peaceful illustrations highlight families and children playing.

Bread, Bread, Bread | Ann Morris; photos by Ken Heyman

Open up this book's cover for a global tour of bread. From the streets of France to a store in Hong Kong, discover over two dozen ways different countries in the world make this staple food. A photographic index follows to let parents know where each type of bread comes from. *Warning: Don't read when hungry!*

Make sure you check out the other titles in this series: *Houses and Homes; Shoes, Shoes, Shoes; Hats, Hats, Hats; On the Go; Tools; Families.*

Can You Say Peace? | Karen Katz

Kids around the world call for peace in this colorful title. Each lefthand page shows a child busy with his or her family and life in a different country. The righthand side explains how he or she pronounces the word for *peace.* On the final page, all the kids wave goodbye from a map of their respective homes.

Children Around the World | Donata Montanari

With sparse text ideal for littles, this book introduces twelve children from around the globe (United States, Canada, Mexico, Bolivia, Morocco, Tanzania, Greece, India, China, Japan, Philippines, and Australia). Colors and textures in the collage artwork make the images appealing. I remember my Trishna saved up and bought a copy of this book with her own money! *Note: Religious beliefs briefly mentioned*

The Colors of Us | Karen Katz

This fun tribute celebrates the diversity of cultures within the United States. Seven-year-old Lena wants to paint her unique skin tone in a portrait, and as she walks through the neighborhood with her mother, she's reminded that everyone has their own special color.

GLOBAL PERSPECTIVE

How do you give your children the world in your home?

"We have couch surfers and exchange students stay with us, and we're learning a foreign language as a family. My husband and I plan trips together and discuss world events with each other in front of the kids—answering their age appropriate questions." Lana, Oklahoma

A Cool Drink of Water | Barbara Kerley

Full-page photos of children and adults showcase the beauty of water around the world: where we get it (a river, a fountain, a well), how we store and carry it (in bottles, bags, pots), and how we love to drink it. Certainly "a nice, cool drink of water" appeals to everyone, no matter where we live. A note at the end of the book mentions the importance of conservation.

How to Make an Apple Pie and See the World | Marjorie Priceman

If the market is open, it's not hard to buy the ingredients needed for apple pie. But what happens when the market closes? You just might find yourself in England for butter, Vermont for apples, and Sri Lanka for cinnamon. A happy read, and if you have a sweet tooth, you'll love the apple pie recipe included at the end!

Little Humans | Brandon Stanton

The founder of the popular *Humans of New York* blog created this diverse celebration of city life for young children. The text is simple, but the photos are multicultural showstoppers that your littles will love checking out.

Me on the Map | Joan Sweeney; illustrated by Annette Cable

This delightful introduction to maps for youngsters invites them to watch a girl show off the maps of her room, street, town, state, country, and world. Then they follow her back again: from her world to her street to her room as she reminds them that every child occupies their own special corner of the map.

One World, One Day | Barbara Kerley

Written by an ex–Peace Corps volunteer, *One World* shows what an entire day from sunrise to sunset looks like for kids around the globe. Stunning photos of school, homework, play, family, and that international question "What's for dinner?" emphasize the parts of life we share. Descriptive pages at the end of the book explain where each photo originated and offer notes from the photographers.

Over the Hills and Far Away: A Treasury of Nursery Rhymes from Around the World | Collected by Elizabeth Hammill

This imaginative collection of multicultural rhymes belongs on the shelf of any home with littles inside! British, American, Chinese, Latino, and African poems (as well as those from other cultures) appear on the pages, paired with illustrations from more than seventy artists. A gorgeous compilation—read one every morning at breakfast to start your day off with poetry!

The Peace Book | Todd Parr

The words *silly* and *fun* perfectly describe these brightly colored pages, with drawings similar to kids' own stick figures, and skin colors that include blue, green, and orange. Diversity in people and animals comes through loud and clear in this lighthearted look at languages, clothes, music, and life around the world.

The Red Book | Barbara Lehman—Caldecott Honor

We can contribute to our children's heart for the world when they're young by stirring up their sense of adventure, which is exactly what this wordless, magical picture book does. The red book in this story transports a girl over oceans and unknown lands to a surprising destination, and it doesn't stop there.

Somewhere in the World Right Now | Stacey Schuett

Introduce the mystery of time zones through this title that showcases everything going on *right now*, somewhere in the world. A baby kangaroo takes a nap in the afternoon, a girl dreams in her hut, and children dress for school—all in the same moment!

This Is the Way We Go to School: A Book about Children Around the World | Edith Baer; illustrated by Steve Bjorkman

From trains to cable cars, gondolas to skis, buses to bicycles, this worldwide tour shows the many ways kids head to school each morning. The fun format displays our global differences and similarities, and the final map explains where each child comes from. Also look for the follow-up title: *This Is the Way We Eat Our Lunch*.

GLOBAL PERSPECTIVE

How do you give your children the world in your home?

"We have two children that we support through World Vision in Brazil and Niger. We also host missionaries that our church supports or have them over for a meal when they are in town so my kids can hear what life is like in other countries. Lastly, we pack shoeboxes for Operation Christmas Child each year. Then we find out where those boxes go and look up information on that country." Jennifer, California

To Be a Kid | Maya Ajmera & John D. Ivanko

Playing ball, drawing, being silly, learning, spending time with family—it's just what you do when you're a kid. Each page features photos of children from different countries engaged in a similar activity with a caption telling where they live. A gorgeous parade of diversity!

What We Wear: Dressing Up Around the World
Maya Ajmera, Elise Hofer Derstine, & Cynthia Pon

Portraits from all corners of the earth highlight with flair how kids dress up for the busyness of life: school, sports, festivals, and play. Each photograph has a caption telling where it was taken, and the appendix encourages little ones to consider what their own styles of dress say about them.

Whoever You Are | Mem Fox; illustrated by Leslie Staub

Bright illustrations and a rhythmical text introduce kids to other children just like them—with laughs, hopes, families, and love—no matter where they come from. A beautiful read for bedtime that you won't mind repeating!

You and Me Together: Moms, Dads, and Kids Around the World
Barbara Kerley

Naps, meals, cuddles, games—check out all the ways moms and dads spend time with their kids throughout the world. Gorgeous global snapshots and simple prose highlight that *family* means "forever," making this a comforting read for newly adopted children.

MULTICULTURAL BOOKS FOR AGES 6–8

Children from Australia to Zimbabwe: A Photographic Journey Around the World | Maya Ajmera & Anna Rhesa Versola

I adore this book, which takes children on an alphabetical tour around the globe—highlighting one country that begins with each letter. It includes a few paragraphs of introduction about each place as well as a map, flag, interesting facts, and a list of other countries that start with the same letter. Younger kids will enjoy flipping through the pages just to look at the photographs. *Note: Religious beliefs mentioned*

Children Just Like Me: A Unique Celebration of Children Around the World | Anabel & Barnabas Kindersley (published in association with UNICEF)

What memories this book stirs up for me! I enthusiastically ordered a copy when I had toddlers. You could say it's *the* title that kindled my passion to "give my children the world." For years they thumbed through it with sweet, chubby fingers—each page packed with plenty to look at and absorb. Later we went through a season where I'd read aloud a page or two every day. It includes an overview of each continent, then a more detailed entry about a child's life from a specific country. This is one you'll want on your shelf long term! *Note: Religious beliefs briefly mentioned*

Follow That Map! A First Book of Mapping Skills | Scot Ritchie

Consider this an interactive map book as the characters ask readers to use directions, symbols, and a compass rose to help them search for their missing pets. The final page invites kids to create a map of their own bedrooms—an activity my children enjoyed at this age. Keep in mind that an interest in maps naturally leads to an interest in the world!

If You Lived Here: Houses of the World | Giles Laroche

History and architecture combine in this book, which highlights different styles of dwellings—stilt houses, adobe homes, chateaus, log cabins, and more—and explains how people built them, where, when, and why. This interesting title also features stunning 3D-style collage illustrations. (This book will appeal to the 8–10 age group as well.)

If You Were Me and Lived in . . . Series | Carole P. Roman

I wish this colorful overview of the world had been published when my kids were younger! Traditional aspects of a culture, including common kids' names, sports, food, and currency receive a mention. Thus far the series includes India, Mexico, France, South Korea, Australia, Kenya, Norway, Peru, Turkey, Russia, Greece, Portugal, Hungary, and Scotland.

Let's Eat: What Children Eat Around the World | Beatrice Hollyer

Introduce your children to Thembe from South Africa, Luis from Mexico, AA from Thailand, Jordan from France, and Yamini from India—five regular kids growing up in different food cultures. Learn how they buy, grow, and prepare daily cuisine and take a peek at one special "feasting" event in each child's life. Recipes included! *Note: Religious beliefs briefly mentioned*

Magic Tree House Series | Mary Pope Osborne

The Magic Tree House Series escorts your just-learning-to-read child from early readers to the realm of short chapter books. Following central characters Jack and Annie and their magical adventures, readers travel the world and learn basic geography and history at the same time. With over fifty titles to choose from, you won't have trouble finding one on a topic of interest. Since some books touch on disturbing aspects of history, like the sinking of the *Titanic* or the Civil War, I suggest previewing first to find out the right age to share these with your kids.

Also check out the Magic Tree House Fact Checkers, a nonfiction companion series aimed at ages 8–10, which goes into greater detail about specific topics like Ancient Greece, the Pilgrims, the American Revolution, and more.

Maps and Globes | Jack Knowlton; illustrated by Harriett Barton

This beginner's history of maps has resided on our family's shelf for years. From the ancient maps of Babylonia drawn in clay, to maps of a flat Earth (don't fall off!), to the way we use maps today, this title has got you covered. There's even an introduction to latitude and longitude.

My Librarian Is a Camel | Margriet Ruurs

After finishing this book, you'll agree with the librarian in Azerbaijan quoted in its pages, who declares that books are "as important as air or water!" Kids get a glimpse of the floating libraries of Indonesia and the camel bookmobiles of Kenya, with plenty in between. These touching stories serve as a reminder that having access to books is a luxury.

National Geographic Kids Beginner's World Atlas
National Geographic

Make this colorful tome your child's first atlas! It's impossible not to be drawn to its photography and fun facts about each continent. This volume includes over twenty physical and political maps—showing bodies of water, climate, plants, animals, people groups, and languages. Perfect for inviting your kids to fall in love with the world at a young age.

On the Same Day in March: A Tour of the World's Weather
Marilyn Singer; illustrated by Frane Lessac

On the same day in March, it might be snowing, windy, hot, or humid—depending on where you live. This book makes over a dozen stops (from the Texas Panhandle to the Nile Valley) to check in on what girls and boys are wearing and doing in their unique climates.

GLOBAL PERSPECTIVE

How do you give your children the world in your home?

"My husband regularly explores Google Earth with our boys, ages five and four. They love it and can identify all the continents. If we encounter something from a different culture during the day, such as music, a book, or a person from a different country, they will get on Google Earth to find that location. My five-year-old wanted to make a boat and sail it to the ocean. We used Google Earth to find a path along the rivers that would eventually take him there!" Malena, Pennsylvania

P Is for Passport: A World Alphabet | Devin Scillian

Earn a few imaginary stamps in your passport as you take in the wonders of the world through this tour. From learning *hello* in multiple languages to checking out different currencies, there's plenty here to interest your youngsters as you read aloud. Eight- to ten-year-olds will enjoy this book on their own as the sidebars offer more details. *Note: The letter "F" mentions different faiths*

A School Like Mine: A Unique Celebration of Schools Around the World
Published in association with UNICEF

This photographic feast emphasizes the ways in which global schools are similar and different. Each page introduces a new child and describes how he or she learns. Find out fun facts like the number of school hours, what everyone eats for lunch, and how much homework they receive. My kids were happy to see home-schooling represented in one of the entries, since our family homeschools. *Note: Religious beliefs briefly mentioned*

Throw Your Tooth on the Roof: Tooth Traditions from Around the World
Selby Beeler; illustrated by G. Brian Karas

If your child lived in Cameroon, he wouldn't put his tooth under the pillow when it fell out, no way. Everyone knows he would throw his tooth over the roof! Your children will laugh out loud as they learn how different countries deal with a lost tooth—whether it's dancing around it, feeding it to the dog, or turning it into an earring.

Where Do I Live? | Neil Chesanow; illustrated by Ann Iosa
Readers gain a basic understanding of geography through this title, which begins in a child's bedroom, then slowly zooms out to his street, town, continent, solar system, and even galaxy. It inspires a sense of wonder at this planet we call home—even my older kids enjoyed it. *Note: These pages mention "your country" when referring to the United States*

MULTICULTURAL BOOKS FOR AGES 8–10

Amelia to Zora: 26 Women Who Changed the World
Cynthia Chin-Lee; illustrated by Megan Halsey & Sean Addy

Come meet a collection of female influencers, both well known and more obscure, who are pioneers in their unique fields. From Mother Teresa to Helen Keller, Oprah to Grace Hopper who discovered the first "computer bug" (yes, a real bug!), this read inspires both daughters and sons. I loved the quotes included from each woman.

A Child's Introduction to the World: Geography, Cultures, and People
Heather Alexander; illustrated by Meredith Hamilton

Did you know placing your hands above your head in greeting is an insult in certain places? I learned so many interesting facts in this cultural introduction, which features watercolor maps, background information on dozens of countries, the history of early explorers, and greetings from around the world. The 2010 edition includes a pop-up paper globe and stickers.

Children Just Like Me: Celebrations | Anabel & Barnabas Kindersley

This husband and wife author/photographer team spent a year traveling the world to compile the sequel to *Children Just Like Me*. This installment has all the enticements of the first—gorgeous photos and full sidebars with plenty of details—but I've placed it in an older age category because many of the festivals and feasts are religious in nature. These pages open the door for discussions about how those around the world believe. *Note: Religious beliefs mentioned*

Christmas Around the World
Mary D. Lankford; illustrated by Karen Dugan

Covering traditions in a dozen countries, this book helps readers learn what people in each place eat, wear (including a description of the holiday forecast), and do to celebrate. Every chapter begins with a history of the country, and the book ends with directions for a handful of crafts—like Filipino parols (stars), British Christmas crackers, and Swedish advent calendars. *Note: Explains the pagan roots of some holiday traditions*

The Golden Rule | Ilene Cooper; illustrated by Gabi Swiatkowska

A boy and his grandfather pass a billboard that reads, "Do unto others as you would have them do unto you." When the boy wonders what it means, his grandfather answers by retelling the golden rule in the words of a variety of faiths, showing that it's an ideal we all have in common. *Note: Religious beliefs mentioned*

If the World Were a Village: A Book about the World's People
David J. Smith; illustrated by Shelagh Armstrong

Make the concept of world population easier to grasp by imagining Earth as one village of a hundred people. In this global village, where does each person come from, how many go to school, how old are they? The book leads to deep thought on an abstract issue. *Note: Religious beliefs briefly mentioned*

The Kids' Multicultural Cookbook | Deanna Cook

Give your geography studies a hands-on element with this cookbook's seventy-five recipes from forty countries. Each recipe includes a difficulty rating, so you can match it to the age of your child and/or how much time you have in the kitchen. The ingredients aren't too exotic and should be easy to find in most supermarkets. Besides the food, your budding chef will also learn about global games and rituals.

The Kingfisher Atlas of World History | Simon Adams

After a quick read of this title, I promptly ordered our own copy. This is one for your shelves—with maps, illustrations, photos, and sidebar timelines that cover historical periods from BC to 2010. So much to look at and learn from! I appreciated that even wars were handled tastefully and not described graphically. Your six- to eight-year-olds may want to flip through as well, just be sure to preview it first. And your ten- to twelve-year-olds will continue using this title for reference.
Note: Religious beliefs mentioned

GLOBAL PERSPECTIVE

How do you give your children the world in your home?

"We have a world map on the wall above our dinner table. We play games like 'What's the capital of . . . ?' or 'I spy a country in the Southern Hemisphere that is purple.' We also support two native missionaries in India, read their newsletters, and pray for them regularly." Rachael, North Carolina

---

A Life Like Mine: How Children Live Around the World
Published in association with UNICEF

These beautiful photographs feature global children and their homes, schools, toys, and families. Keep in mind that it also addresses heavy issues like child labor, war, malnutrition, and disease—making this a better fit for slightly older readers.
Note: Religious beliefs mentioned. Includes an entire section on war and how it affects children, with photos of tanks and a few weapons.

Loaves of Fun: A History of Bread with Activities and Recipes from Around the World
Elizabeth M. Harbison; illustrated by John Harbison

We come from different places with vastly different cultures and daily lives. But we have at least one thing in common: bread! This fun title uses a timeline format to explore the origin of bread around the world—from its start in Mesopotamia, to its journey through Rome and other empires, to our modern ways of preparing it today. Plenty of recipes for your hands-on learners (and tasters)!

Maps | Aleksandra Mizielinska & Daniel Mizielinski

If you've ever thought of maps as art, this book is an absolute must-have! Each continent (and several countries on it) has its own oversized two-page map spread, bursting with illustrations of the historical details and other well-known facts from that location. For example, the map of Italy has drawings of Caesar, Pinocchio, the leaning tower of Pisa, tiramisu, Dante, and more. *Note: Religious beliefs briefly mentioned*

Off to Class: Incredible and Unusual Schools Around the World
Susan Hughes

My kids kept disappearing with this book, and it was all I could do to get it back. They thought it very cool that a homeschooling family like ours was listed among all the other "incredible" schools! The book showcases dozens of ways to learn—from boats in Bangladesh during flooding season, to tents in Haiti after the earthquake, to even a school on wheels in India that goes to children who don't have access to education any other way. *Note: Religious beliefs mentioned*

The Story of the World | Susan Wise Bauer

This four-volume series chronicles Earth's history from ancient times to the end of the USSR. Written in a captivating narrative perfect for reading aloud, children can't help but engage with this dramatic real-life story of our planet. Be sure to look for the audio version, fabulously performed by storyteller Jim Weiss. *Note: Religious beliefs mentioned*

Titles in the series:
- Volume 1. *Ancient Times: From the Earliest Nomads to the Last Roman Emperor*
- Volume 2. *The Middle Ages: From the Fall of Rome to the Rise of the Renaissance*

- Volume 3. *Early Modern Times: From Elizabeth the First to the Forty-Niners*
- Volume 4. *The Modern Age: From Victoria's Empire to the End of the USSR*

Talking Walls: Discover Your World
Margy Burns Knight; illustrated by Anne Silbey O'Brien

Historical walls and what they teach us form this book's premise, which begins with the Great Wall of China and leads readers to aboriginal caves, Diego Rivera's murals in Mexico, the Vietnam Veterans Memorial, the Berlin Wall, and the jail cell that tried to hold Nelson Mandela. Fascinating! *Note: Religious beliefs mentioned*

MULTICULTURAL BOOKS FOR AGES 10–12

10 Girls/Boys Who Changed the World | Irene Howat

Trishna recently mentioned that she might like to be a missionary someday, so I ordered the girls' version of this book for her. She enthusiastically told me about each chapter, which highlights a female missionary (such as Corrie ten Boom, Gladys Aylward, and Amy Carmichael). If your kids enjoy it, look for the others in the series. Just know that some readers have found *Ten Girls/Boys Who Didn't Give In*, which includes martyr stories, too intense. *Note: Written from a Christian perspective*

Girls/Boys Who Rocked the World | Michelle Roehm McCann and Amelie Weldon; illustrated by David Hahn

This series (one title for girls and one for boys) serves up dozens of mini-biographies about individuals who made an impact on the world before the age of twenty. Mixing historical figures with contemporary ones and famous influencers with those lesser known, this collection includes Galileo, Crazy Horse, Bruce Lee, Mother Teresa, Coco Chanel, and Joan of Arc—to name a few! *Note: Religious beliefs mentioned*

The International Cookbook for Kids | Matthew Locricchio

Few things thrill me more as a parent than seeing my kids busy at work in the kitchen (providing they also clean up the mess!). This global volume packs in over sixty recipes from four parts of the world well known for their flavors: Italy, France, China, and Mexico. The author emphasizes the importance of cooking from scratch with fresh, organic ingredients—it's a cooking course and a geography lesson in one! After you've read it, check out *The 2nd International Cookbook for Kids* and cook your way through India, Greece, Thailand, and Brazil.

National Geographic Kids World Atlas | National Geographic

Expect National Geographic to do what they do best here—detailed charts, stunning photography, and interesting statistics, all aimed at a tween audience. On top of a plethora of world and continent maps to pore over, there's also in-depth information on each ocean, bonus mobile content to download, and a section of games to puzzle over in the appendix. *Note: Religious beliefs mentioned*

GLOBAL PERSPECTIVE

How do you give your children the world in your home?

"I specifically look for books about different cultures when we go to the library. A global perspective is so important because that is how we learn to be human; having compassion and understanding for different view points and customs even if they are drastically different from ours! I want my kids to grow up open-minded and full of curiosity and love, not haters of things they fear or don't understand." Callie, South Dakota

---

Paths to Peace: People Who Changed the World | Jane Bresken Zalben

Profiling sixteen individuals who brought peace to our planet, this collection contains a one-page overview of each hero as well as unique collage artwork and quotes. There's a nice balance of both men and women, from close to home and far away—including Emerson, Gandhi, Einstein, Anne Frank, the Dalai Lama, Aung San Suu Kyi, and more. A moving read for tweens! *Note: Religious beliefs mentioned*

Stories to Solve: Fifteen Folktales from Around the World
George Shannon; illustrated by Peter Sis

A book of global folktales with a twist, each chapter in *Stories to Solve* features a mystery: Why would it be helpful to arrest a stone? How can a crow drink from an empty dish? You find the solution after turning the page. A section of notes explains where each story originated. Look for two more volumes in this series if your kids like the first! *Note: One story mentions heaven and hell*

What the World Eats | Faith D'Aluisio; photographs by Peter Menzel

What do you eat in a whole week? That's the question this author-and-photographer team set out to answer as they traveled to twenty-one countries and took a picture of a family surrounded by the amount of food they consume in seven days. The differences are shocking—my kids and I were stunned by the photo of the Aboubakar family in Chad, who spend just $1.22 a week to feed their family of six. The author also addresses fast-food culture, life expectancy, and growing obesity rates. *Note: Religious beliefs mentioned as they relate to food*

Heroes in History Series and Christian Heroes: Then and Now Series
Janet and Geoff Benge

Published by Youth With A Mission, these captivating series for tweens have been two of Jonathan's favorites for years. The Heroes in History set contains over twenty titles with biographies of famous presidents, inventors, and notable history-makers like George Washington Carver, Meriwether Lewis, Harriet Tubman, Clara Barton, Laura Ingalls Wilder, and Billy Graham.

The Christian Heroes Series, with over forty titles by the same authors, tells the life stories of well-known world-changers including William Booth, John Wesley, Jim and Elisabeth Elliot, and Brother Andrew. *Note: Both series written from a Christian perspective. We've noticed that the Christian Heroes Series occasionally contains violence that might disturb sensitive readers; I suggest previewing first.*

CHAPTER 6

BRING THE RAIN: AFRICA

Countries/regions included in this chapter: Benin, Chad, East Africa, Ethiopia, Ghana, Kenya, Liberia, Malawi, Mali, Nigeria, Rwanda, South Africa, Sudan, Tanzania, Uganda, West Africa, Zambia, Zimbabwe

Something about Africa changes you. If you've ever visited the continent, you know what I mean. Its beauty and its need can't help but make an impact. I've only been once, when I first met Elijah, yet I left part of my heart behind. That's why it blesses me to see just how much my son loves his cultural identity as a Liberian and takes pride in his heritage. Africa is deep in his soul.

Until we can return together, we've used many of the books on the list that follows to keep us connected with this place that will forever remain an important part of our family. There's so much to discover and learn through these titles—enjoy exploring them with your loved ones.

AFRICAN BOOKS FOR AGES 4-6

Rain School (Chad) | James Rumford

Eager children walk to their first day of school, imagining the education they'll receive or simply hoping for their first pencils. But when they arrive, there's no school building. The teacher tells them that constructing the classroom will be their first lesson. A year of enthusiastic learning follows as they work together.

Jambo Means Hello: Swahili Alphabet Book (East Africa)
Muriel Feelings; illustrated by Tom Feelings—Caldecott Honor

Proceeding through the alphabet, each page of this book begins with a letter and word used to describe East African culture. Lovely black-and-white drawings add depth to the short text. I learned so much from this read!

Moja Means One: A Swahili Counting Book (East Africa)
Muriel Feelings; illustrated by Tom Feelings—Caldecott Honor

This title presents numbers one through ten in Swahili, along with their pronunciation and a cultural description. Mount Kilimanjaro, traditional clothing styles, the Nile, and much more make an appearance in this East African introduction.

Bringing the Rain to Kapiti Plain (Kenya) | Verna Aardema

Cow-herder Ki-pat saves his land from an extended drought by shooting a feather into an overhanging dark cloud, bringing the rain to Kapiti Plain. Mirroring the cadence of the British nursery rhyme "The House That Jack Built," the build-up of rhyme and repetition in this book adds to the fun for young listeners.

GLOBAL PERSPECTIVE

How do you give your children the world in your home?

"Our family celebrates different festivals. We draw inspiration from our cultural heritage, immigrant groups in our area, and the places family and friends live around the world. For each festival, I choose a story or book, a craft, a song, a recipe, and some sort of activity, which the whole family participates in. Not only are we learning about geography, culture, and history, but I hope I'm also sowing seeds of peace. We spend quality time together as a family, and we get to realise that, although we may do things differently, essentially our dreams of hope and freedom and our sentiments of gratitude are the same the world over." Tania, United Kingdom

For You Are a Kenyan Child (Kenya)
Kelly Cunnane; illustrated by Ana Juan

Grandfather asks his grandson to care for the herd of cows during the day, but the village distractions pull the boy away from his responsibility. There's too much to see and do—until Grandfather's gentle reprimand prompts him to head back where he belongs. Charming illustrations add to this sweet day-in-the-life story.

Papa, Do You Love Me? (Kenya) | Barbara Joosse & Barbara Lavallee

A Maasai father promises to unconditionally love, protect, and provide for his son. No matter what obstacle comes against them—drought, wild animals, or heat—the father promises that his great love will overcome any challenge. Includes a helpful glossary of cultural terms from the story.

Wangari's Trees of Peace: A True Story from Africa (Kenya)
Jeanette Winter

Disturbed by the deforestation she finds in her Kenyan homeland after returning from America, Wangari doesn't complain. Instead she gets to work—planting nine small seedlings in her backyard. Her growing vision inspires women throughout the country, who join her efforts to add green back to the suffering landscape. *Note: I've included four books about Wangari in this reading list. Each tells her powerful story from a slightly different angle, suitable for a specific age group.*

Two Ways to Count to Ten: A Liberian Folktale (Liberia)
Ruby Dee; illustrated by Susan Meddaugh

King Leopard must find the best animal in the jungle to marry his daughter and inherit the kingdom. He arranges a contest—whichever beast can throw a spear and count to ten before it returns to earth will win. Many animals compete, only to discover in the end that wit matters more than strength. We often read this book aloud every year when we celebrate Elijah's Liberia Day!

At the Crossroads (South Africa) | Rachel Isadora

The village boys journey to the crossroads to wait for their fathers, coming home after ten months working in the mines. Many other villagers join in the day's anticipation, but as the hours slowly pass by, only the dedicated sons remain. Will their fathers ever arrive? A heartwarming tale about love and family with illustrations so moving they brought tears to this mama's eyes.

Lala Salama: A Tanzanian Lullaby (Tanzania)
Patricia MacLachlan; illustrated by Elizabeth Zunon

This sweet story follows mama and baby from morning to nightfall in Tanzania—watching from the shore for their baba's (father's) boat to return. Throughout the day the same refrain repeats: "Lala salama"—dream your dreams. Peaceful drawings of loving family scenes will touch your heart.

We All Went on Safari: A Counting Journey Through Tanzania (Tanzania)
Laurie Krebs; illustrated by Julia Cairns

Simple text and rhythm make this book a perfect Tanzanian introduction for young listeners, who journey alongside a tribe as they cross the Serengeti plain. Learn about the Maasai, African animals, counting from one to ten, and Swahili in this easy read.

Anansi and the Moss-Covered Rock (West Africa)
Eric Kimmel; illustrated by Janet Stevens

In this traditional West African folktale, trickster Anansi the spider determines to pull one over on his animal friends. But in the end, timid Little Bush Deer uses the magic moss-covered rock to teach Anansi a lesson.

Where Are You Going, Manyoni? (Zimbabwe) | Catherine Stock
Manyoni lives far from her school and must start the day early due to the long walk. Along the way she passes many native trees and animals beginning their own day. A helpful page at the end includes a list of unfamiliar words, their pronunciations, and meanings. The watercolors vividly bring the countryside to life.

AFRICAN BOOKS FOR AGES 6–8

A Is for Africa (Africa) | Ifeoma Onyefulu
Filled with large, full-color photos from an African village, *A Is for Africa* proceeds through the alphabet, using each letter as a connection to an aspect of daily life. Though the photos all come from Nigeria, the author has carefully chosen customs that represent other parts of the continent as well. *Note: Religious beliefs mentioned*

Africa Is Not a Country (Africa)
Margy Burns Knight; illustrated by Anne Sibley O'Brien

Each country in Africa has its own unique culture and traditions, a fact sometimes overlooked. This book celebrates those differences, offering snapshots of children and families in various locations on the continent. Includes an index with specific details about each nation. *Note: Religious beliefs mentioned*

Anna Hibiscus (Africa) | Atinuke; illustrated by Lauren Tobia

In this early chapter book, we meet Anna Hibiscus, who lives in amazing Africa with her Canadian mother, African father, and twin baby brothers: Double and Trouble. Her mischievous exploits and childlike adventures bring to mind the classic *Milly Molly Mandy*. If your kids fall in love with Anna, look for others in the series!

Elephants of Africa (Africa) | Gail Gibbons

This title combines drawings of elephants with basic facts and figures about them. Young readers learn how elephants use their teeth, skin, eyes, and ears, how they play together and find food and water, as well as about efforts to protect their habitats from poachers and other threats.

Jaha and Jamil Went Down the Hill: An African Mother Goose (Africa)
Virginia Kroll; illustrated by Katherine Roundtree

Classic Mother Goose rhymes receive an African twist in this sweet book—including "Jack and Jill," "Pease Porridge Hot," "To Market, To Market," and dozens more. Each short verse mirrors the cadence of its traditional counterpart. Clever!

Why the Sun and the Moon Live in the Sky: An African Folktale (Africa)
Elphinstone Dayrell; illustrated by Blair Lent

Sun and Water want to see each other more often, but Water and his people always flow too rapidly to fit in Sun's house. Sun and his wife, Moon, decide to build a larger home to accommodate them. When he finally comes to visit, Water brings so many friends that Sun and Moon must find another new dwelling place—the sky.

GLOBAL PERSPECTIVE

How do you give your children the world in your home?

"We live 45 minutes outside of New York City and try to take advantage of the world there. Probably our favorite way to introduce our kids to various cultures is through food. My kids are pretty picky eaters but have been willing to try food (as long as it isn't too spicy)—from Turkey, India, and Ethiopia. We also try and talk to people in our community about where they are from (when they have an accent) and ask them questions about their home country." Kiasa, New York

---

The Best Beekeeper of Lalibela: A Tale from Africa (Ethiopia)
Cristina Kessler; illustrated by Leonard Jenkins

Legend has it that the city of Lalibela produces Ethiopia's sweetest, tastiest honey. Young Almaz samples it each week at the market, where she decides that one day she will make the best honey of all. The male beekeepers laugh and tease, but Almaz gathers strength from her priest, who encourages her never to give up. In the end, she proves herself to the entire city. *Note: Religious beliefs briefly mentioned*

E Is for Ethiopia (Ethiopia) | Ashenafi Gudeta; photographs by Ashenafi Gudeta, Athklti Mulu, Betelhem Abate & Dama Boru

Vibrant full-color photos fill this book, which presents each letter of the alphabet (A for Aheya—meaning "donkey"; C for famous Ethiopian coffee) alongside a description of the country's culture and history. *Note: Religious belief briefly mentioned*

Mama Miti: Wangari Maathai and the Trees of Kenya (Kenya)
Donna Jo Napoli; illustrated by Kadir Nelson

Poor women all over Kenya travel long distances to speak with wise Wangari, who gives them a specific tree to solve their troubles—such as lack of food, sick animals, or a need for firewood. As more women get involved, the landscape is transformed and the people revitalized. Based on the true story of the first African woman to ever win a Nobel Peace Prize.

Mama Panya's Pancakes (Kenya)
Mary & Rich Chamberlin; illustrated by Julia Cairns

Mama Panya and her son, Adika, walk to market and discuss their plan to make pancakes. On the journey, the friendly boy invites nearly everyone he meets to join them, while Mama Panya counts her coins and worries she won't have enough to share. Yet when the neighbors arrive, each contributes in their own way—making for a lavish feast with plenty left over. A lovely lesson on the benefits of generosity.

Planting the Trees of Kenya: The Story of Wangari Maathai (Kenya)
Claire Nivola

Wangari's mother taught her to respect nature, so it shocks Wangari upon returning from studies abroad to find Kenya in disarray: the land barren of trees, the people struggling. Wangari takes action planting trees and inviting others—including women, children, and even soldiers—to do the same. Along the way, she impacts millions of lives.

Who's in Rabbit's House? (Kenya/Tanzania)
Verna Aardema; illustrated by Leo & Diane Dillon

Maasai villagers gather to watch their friends and family perform a play in which the actors try to figure out who has taken over Rabbit's house! It certainly sounds like a vicious animal, and Frog must come to the rescue after larger creatures like Elephant, Rhino, and Leopard fail to help.

The Boy Who Harnessed the Wind (Malawi)
William Kamkwamba & Bryan Mealer; illustrated by Elizabeth Zunon

When poverty forces William to drop out of school, he takes up his own education at the library—researching solutions to make his community stronger. William eventually transforms his drought-stricken village by creating a windmill from scraps of junk to harness wind power for electricity and water. An incredible true story.

Galimoto (Malawi) | Karen Lynn Williams; illustrated by Catherine Stock
Seven-year-old Kondi desperately wants to make his own galimoto—a toy crafted out of wire. But he doesn't have the right supplies. His brother laughs at his efforts, and Kondi faces plenty of obstacles in the village. Yet he finally proves that with determination you can accomplish whatever you set out to do.

I Lost My Tooth in Africa (Mali)
Penda Diakité; illustrated by Baba Wague Diakité

Amina discovers her loose tooth just before the plane lands in Mali. Hearing that the African Tooth Fairy will give her a chicken in exchange, she shouts for joy when the tooth later falls out by the papaya tree. This story praises the closeness of family, the comfort found in daily routines, and the thrill of childhood milestones. I love the authenticity of the drawings, created by the author's West African father.

The Day Gogo Went to Vote (South Africa)
Eleanor Batezat Sisulu; illustrated by Sharon Wilson

Thembi's elderly grandmother, Gogo, shocks the family with her intention to vote in the upcoming election. Though she hasn't left home for years, Gogo refuses to miss participating in the first poll opened to black South Africans. Six-year-old Thembi travels along, offering a child's perspective on this historic event.

The Dove (South Africa) | Dianne Stewart; illustrated by Jude Daly
Grandmother Maloko cannot plant her crops until the rain ends—yet the great flood goes on and on. When the sun finally peeks through the clouds, her granddaughter Lindi emerges from the house and sees a single dove. The bird becomes both a symbol of hope and the practical inspiration to supply their needs as they wait for the ground to dry.

The Gift of the Sun: A Tale from South Africa (South Africa)
Dianne Stewart; illustrated by Jude Daly

Thulani would rather sit in the sun than milk the cow or do any work on his farm. In an attempt to simplify, he sells the cow and brings home a goat instead. This sets off a cycle of one trade after another, eventually resulting in a transformed Thulani and a fortune too.

Goal! (South Africa) | Mina Javaherbin; illustrated by A. G. Ford
Ajani wins a shiny soccer ball for being the best reader in his class. His friends gather joyfully after school to play in the dusty alley, but the streets are dangerous. Soon bullies stop the game and threaten to steal the prize. Ajani and his teammates have to think fast to keep themselves, and their treasured ball, safe.

My Painted House, My Friendly Chicken, and Me (South Africa)
Maya Angelou; photographs by Margaret Courtney-Clarke

Thandi lives in a South African tribe with her family and her best friend, a chicken. She loves her village's tradition of colorfully painting their huts. When visiting a nearby city, the girl feels sorry for those who live in boring houses that look alike. Maya Angelou's words join with stunning photographs to bring Thandi's treasured huts alive.

Babu's Song (Tanzania)
Stephanie Stuve-Bodeen; illustrated by Aaron Boyd

More than anything, Bernardi wishes he could buy the ball he saw in a local shop. But living with his grandfather Babu, the boy can't even afford to go to school. One day a tourist offers to buy a homemade music box Babu gave him. Should Bernardi sell it and spend the earnings? An inspirational read about priorities and using money wisely.

My Rows and Piles of Coins (Tanzania)
Tololwa Mollel; illustrated by E. B. Lewis

Saruni saves the coins he earns from helping his mother at the market each week, hoping to buy a bicycle to carry loads back and forth for the family. Though he doesn't end up with enough, his dream comes true in an unexpected way—a beautiful reminder of how the right motive does not go unrewarded.

GLOBAL PERSPECTIVE
How do you give your children the world in your home?

"Our family sponsors multiple children through Compassion International. Each of my girls has a "birthday buddy" who they write to monthly. We have also traveled as a family to meet one of our sponsored children. As often as possible, we have people from other countries and cultures to our home for dinner. We've had Alex from Uganda, Marlennis from Dominican Republic, Ariel from Honduras, Meerko from Germany, and more." Jill, Oregon

Beatrice's Goat (Uganda)
Page McBrier; illustrated by Lori Lohstoeter

Beatrice hopes to attend school, but her family lacks the needed funds. Then her mother receives a goat as a gift. Beatrice soon realizes that the animal, whose name means "luck," lives up to her promise—offering the girl a chance at an education. A book that celebrates hard work and provision!

Uncommon Traveler: Mary Kingsley in Africa (West Africa)
Don Brown

Eight-year-old Mary Kingsley lives mostly alone—with only her bedridden mother and her books—in a gloomy house outside London. She devours tales of travel and adventure and shocks everyone at the age of thirty by moving to West Africa. A true story of courage, passion, and finding your place in the world.

AFRICAN BOOKS FOR AGES 8-10

African Critters (Africa) | Robert Haas

Journey alongside National Geographic's photographer during a day on a wildlife photo shoot. Discover leopards, elephants, wild dogs, lions, and more in these pages as Haas shares the animals' stories as well as his passion for conservation and the environment.

Ashanti to Zulu: African Traditions (Africa) | Margaret Musgrove; illustrated by Diane & Leo Dillon—Caldecott Medal

In this picture book, author Margaret Musgrove describes the characteristics and cultures of twenty-six African tribes. Details of daily life, special rituals, and celebrations combined with full-color illustrations make this Caldecott Medal winner an educational read. *Note: Religious beliefs mentioned*

Fire on the Mountain (Ethiopia) | Jane Kurtz; illustrated by E. B. Lewis

Alemayu imagines himself with plenty of money, yet he spends his days working as a shepherd boy. When his parents die, he seeks refuge with his sister, a cook in the home of a rich man. The wealthy master gives Alemayu a challenge—spend an entire night alone on the cold mountain—and either make a fortune or perish in the attempt.

One Hen: How One Small Loan Made a Big Difference (Ghana)
Katie Smith Milway; illustrated by Eugenie Fernandes

The village gives Kojo's mother a small loan, enough to buy a cart to haul fire-wood as well as one hen. Within a year, the boy manages to grow his flock of hens to twenty-five. He enrolls in school, studies hard, and expands his business. Eventually his farm becomes the largest in West Africa, and Kojo starts offering loans to others. Inspired by a true story, this is a perfect introduction to the concept of microfinance.

Seven Spools of Thread (Ghana)
Angela Shelf Medearis; illustrated by Daniel Minter

Originally created as a Kwanzaa story, this picture book is a perfect read-aloud any time of year for families struggling with sibling rivalry. Seven constantly quarreling brothers are given an impossible task after their father dies: to make gold out of seven spools of colored thread. By nurturing peace instead of strife with each other, they find that even the unattainable lies within their reach.

GLOBAL PERSPECTIVE

How do you give your children the world in your home?

"We have family who are missionaries in South Africa—so we talk about what they do, and why they live there. We sponsor a child in Rwanda through Compassion who writes and tells us about the reality of his life. This has caused our eldest to have a really compassionate heart. We have plans to travel to different cultures, but for now we read stories and watch movies to try to get a taste." Bethany, United Kingdom

14 Cows for America (Kenya)
Carmen Agra Deedy; illustrated by Thomas Gonzalez

Kimeli has spent years away from his Maasai tribe, studying in New York City. Upon his return, he sadly tells his friends about the tragedy of September 11. The villagers decide to donate their most precious and treasured possessions—fourteen cows. A diplomat from the U.S. embassy in Nairobi attends the sacred ceremony in which the cows are blessed as a measure of comfort and peace for

America. *14 Cows for America* includes an afterword from Wilson Kimeli Naiyomah, the Maasai warrior at the heart of this gorgeous book.

Owen & Mzee: The True Story of a Remarkable Friendship (Kenya)
Isabella and Craig Hatkoff & Paula Kahumbu;
photographs by Peter Greste

In the wake of the 2004 tsunami in Southeast Asia, a baby hippo that came to be known as Owen was separated from his family. After his rescue, a 130-year-old giant tortoise called Mzee unexpectedly "adopts" him. This book tells the full story, including snapshots of this unlikely pair snuggling together!

Seeds of Change: Wangari's Gift to the World (Kenya)
Jen Cullerton Johnson; illustrated by Sonia Lynn Sadler

Though few girls in her tribe receive an education, Wangari longs to learn. In school she discovers her passion for science and leaves to study in the United States. Upon her return, she begins a campaign to plant trees, which comes to be known as the Green Belt Movement. This version of Wangari's story highlights her firsts as a female scientist and the unique struggles she had to face to complete her mission.

Why the Sky Is Far Away: A Nigerian Folktale (Nigeria)
Mary-Joan Gerson; illustrated by Carla Golembe

In this retelling of a traditional myth, the sky was once close enough for villagers to eat. But over time the people begin to waste it, taking more than needed and discarding the excess. After an unheeded warning, the sky moves away, requiring the community to work the land for their food instead. Combine this read with a discussion about responsible stewardship. *Note: Religious beliefs of the Bini Tribe mentioned*

Gorilla Doctors: Saving Endangered Great Apes (Rwanda/Uganda)
Pamela Turner

Discover an endangered species and learn about the scientists helping them. Mountain gorillas face threats from poachers and even tourists, who have unknowingly brought human diseases into their population. Dozens of photographs bring these playful, curious animals to life—and explain the measures being taken to save them.

Nelson Mandela: Long Walk to Freedom (South Africa)
editor Chris van Wyk; illustrated by Paddy Bouma

This edited version of Mandela's autobiography gives readers a shocking glimpse into apartheid. Beginning with his childhood in a traditional village, it covers Mandela's schooling, his involvement in social justice and equality efforts, his imprisonment and eventual freedom. An absolute wealth of information about South Africa's history.

GLOBAL PERSPECTIVE

How do you give your children the world in your home?

"Being an Active Duty Army family, a global perspective comes with the territory! We have had neighbors from all over the world and have lived in Europe and many different states. My kids have traveled to Israel and Africa, and we have friends who are missionaries in different parts of the world. We have always tried to learn about the history and culture of wherever we are through books, field trips, and activities, as well as just living with our neighbors." Holly, Texas

---

Peaceful Protest: The Life of Nelson Mandela (South Africa)
Yona Zeldis McDonough; illustrated by Malcah Zeldis

Featuring unique, bold, and colorful illustrations, this picture-book account of Nelson Mandela opens with his birth and proceeds through his life until his historic election as president of South Africa.

Why Mosquitoes Buzz in People's Ears: A West African Tale (West Africa)
Verna Aardema; illustrated by Diane & Leo Dillon—Caldecott Medal

Why won't Mother Owl wake the sun so the day can begin? The jungle animals play a game of pass the buck to find out who is responsible for Owl's tardiness, eventually resting the blame on the mosquito—which explains why she continues buzzing in ears to this day.

Mufaro's Beautiful Daughters (Zimbabwe)
John Steptoe—Caldecott Honor

Mufaro has two beautiful daughters—one selfish, one thoughtful. Bitter, ill-tempered Manyara grumbles constantly, while kind Nyasha serves willingly. One day a messenger arrives, announcing that the king seeks a wife. All daughters may appear before him. Both girls make their way to the city only to find selflessness rewarded in the end. *Note: Religious beliefs mentioned*

AFRICAN BOOKS FOR AGES 10-12

Nelson Mandela's Favorite African Folktales (Africa)
edited by Nelson Mandela

This collection of thirty-two popular folktales includes creation stories, animal fables, and good-versus-evil legends. Compiled and edited by Nelson Mandela, it also contains a map of Africa, highlighting each story's origin. *Note: Religious beliefs mentioned*

The Kidnapped Prince: The Life of Olaudah Equiano (Benin)
Ann Cameron

Ann Cameron used Equiano's autobiography, published in 1789, to create this accessible version for younger readers, which shines a shocking light on the subject of slavery. Slave-traders kidnap Equiano—the son of an African chief—from his village at the age of eleven. He spends the next decade desperately searching for freedom.

The Storyteller's Beads (Ethiopia)
Jane Kurtz; illustrated by Michael Bryant

Set in Ethiopia in the 1980s, *The Storyteller's Beads* traces the unlikely friendship of two girls—a Christian and a Jew. Cultural and religious prejudices keep Sahey and Rahel enemies until their fight for survival while fleeing the country binds them together. Contains a cultural glossary and afterword that puts the novel into its historical context. *Note: Christian and Jewish beliefs mentioned*

Listening for Lions (Kenya) | Gloria Whelan

Rachel knows no other life than the one she has with her missionary parents in East Africa—until both die from an influenza epidemic. In the midst of her grief, another Western couple whose daughter died forces Rachel to play the part of their own child in order to win a relative's large inheritance. An exciting novel full of deception, adventure, and love of Africa.

Beat the Story-Drum, Pum-Pum (Nigeria) | Ashley Bryan

This collection breathes new life into five Nigerian folktales: "Hen and Frog," "Why Bush Cow and Elephant are Bad Friends," "The Husband Who Counted the Spoonfuls," "Why Frog and Snake Never Play Together," and "How Animals Got Their Tails." The author delivers each legend with rhythmical language—like the beat of a story drum. *Note: Religious beliefs mentioned*

Journey to Jo'burg: A South African Story (South Africa)
Beverley Naidoo; illustrated by Eric Velasquez

Mma works as a white family's maid in Johannesburg, far from her three children. But when their baby sister becomes ill, Naledi and her younger brother, Tiro, decide they must reach their mother immediately. The journey is fraught with danger and difficulty, and when they reach the city, they begin to piece together the reality of life under the confines of apartheid.

Year of No Rain (Sudan) | Alice Mead

Eleven-year-old Stephen lives with his mother and sister in southern Sudan. He hopes to become a teacher, but all dreams are placed on hold the day his family hears gunshots approaching. Expecting rebels who want to kidnap boys as soldiers, his mother sends Stephen to hide. When the boy returns, the entire village has been decimated—his mother has been killed and his sister has disappeared. A story of courage, vision, and loyalty.

GLOBAL PERSPECTIVE

How do you give your children the world in your home?

"We just finished a year of 'traveling' the globe with the aid of a flat paper doll named after our youngest. I sent the doll to several people around the world, and they took photos with her at favorite locations in their countries. We then read stories and fables based in those countries, and explored the music, art, and foods of each place. It was a tremendous year of study." Kimberly, Colorado

My Life with the Chimpanzees (Tanzania) | Jane Goodall

I sat down with this book intending to quickly preview it, yet I soon found myself captivated by Jane Goodall's story, which she shares in this kids' version of her autobiography. She describes in detail her young fascination with all African things and the amazing path that led to her life's calling with the chimps of Tanzania.

Ryan and Jimmy: And the Well in Africa That Brought Them Together (Uganda) | Herb Shoveller

When Canadian first-grader Ryan Hreljac hears about the need for clean water in Africa, he becomes a boy with a mission. What starts with extra chores to earn money leads to an international campaign and a Ugandan village transformed by his efforts. But it doesn't stop there. After Ryan's Ugandan pen pal, Jimmy, gets abducted by rebel forces, Ryan's family starts a long process to bring him to safety. An incredible true story!

The Cow-Tail Switch: And Other West African Stories (West Africa)
Harold Courlander & George Herzog; illustrated
by Madye Lee Chastain—Newbery Honor

This book contains seventeen traditional West African stories—legends and tall tales about animals, kings, and warriors. Well-known creatures like Frog and Rabbit make an appearance, alongside the famous Anansi and Turtle. Especially helpful is a section called Notes on the Stories, explaining the context and culture of each tale's origin. *Note: Religious beliefs mentioned*

Bulu: African Wonder Dog (Zambia) | Dick Houston

Bulu isn't like other dogs. His uniqueness attracts Steve and Anna Tolan, who left England to start over in the wilderness of Zambia. Little do they know that by adopting Bulu, whose name means "wild dog," their lives will change forever. The puppy fills their days with excitement—including animal rescues and lion attacks. Perfect adventure reading!

CHAPTER 7

NUMBER THE STARS: EUROPE

Countries/regions included in this chapter: Austria, Czech Republic, Denmark, England, France, Germany, Greece, Hungary, Iceland, Ireland, Italy, Lithuania, the Netherlands, Norway, Poland, Russia, Scotland, Spain, Sweden, Switzerland

Having a British husband comes with perks, let me tell ya. There's the accent, the tea, the extended family, and the need to travel regularly to visit them. The first time we took the whole family to England together, the kids were nine, eight, and seven. Guess what we used to get ourselves mentally prepared for the trip: books, of course!

During our travels, we wove a few amazing book-related excursions into our stay—a tour of Beatrix Potter's home in the Lake District, a journey to the real Sherwood Forest, and even a personal trip to the Brontë sisters' home in the Yorkshire moors. Europe can be bliss for book lovers, and this list is a perfect place to start your explorations.

EUROPEAN BOOKS FOR AGES 4–6

In the Belly of an Ox: The Unexpected Photographic Adventures of Richard and Cherry Kearton (England) | Rebecca Bond

Brothers Richard and Cherry Kearton spent their childhood in the Yorkshire countryside. Later in life they developed creative camouflaging ideas that allowed them to photograph birds in their habitats up close—producing the first natural history book that included photographs. An inspiring read for nature lovers!

Anno's Journey (Europe) | Mitsumasa Anno

This fascinating wordless picture book takes readers through the landscapes of Northern Europe to watch as residents work and play. Cleverly incorporated in the illustrations are details from famous European paintings, composers, and fairy tales. A note at the end of the book mentions the features to keep an eye out for. Such a cool concept!

Adèle & Simon (France) | Barbara McClintock

Adele picks her younger brother up from school and urges him to carefully hold his things on the way home. One by one, Simon's belongings go missing at each famous city landmark before the children reach their own doorstep. Clever and sweet!

The Cat Who Walked Across France (France)
Kate Banks; illustrated by Georg Hallensleben

The cat used to live happily with a caring old woman, but when the woman died, he needed to find a new home. His quest leads him all the way across the country toward the sea, where he finds exactly what he's been looking for. Lovely illustrations.

GLOBAL PERSPECTIVE

How do you give your children the world in your home?

"We've taken 'living globally' to an extreme . . . in the past seven years we've traveled to or lived in seventeen countries on four continents (#18 and #5 come next month when we head to Morocco) with our (now) six kids . . . we started with just four. We don't have an official home, we sold it all to explore the world, although we are looking for a home base now. We're currently living in Germany, but wondering if France or Italy will be the place to continue our travels from." Rachel

Henri's Walk to Paris (France) | Leonore Klein; illustrated by Saul Bass

Young Henri lives in a small village yet dreams of venturing to the big city of Paris. One day he decides to walk there and get a glimpse of it for himself, but he ends up taking a bit of a wrong turn. Charming!

Kiki and Coco in Paris (France)
Nina Gruener; photographs by Stephanie Rausser

In a global storyline many little ones can relate to, Kiki takes her beloved doll Coco everywhere. They travel the city together—until the doll accidentally gets left behind. Thus begins a scramble, a search, and a happy pair reunited. Includes beautiful photographs of Paris.

Going Fishing (Iceland) | Bruce McMillan

Today young Fridrik is going fishing for the first time. Join the boy and his grandfather on their journey as they catch cod and lumpfish and introduce us to the heart of Iceland—fish on the money, fish on the stamps, fish in the sea.

The Problem with Chickens (Iceland)
Bruce McMillan; illustrated by Gunnella

The ladies of this Icelandic village must have eggs for cooking, so they buy some chickens. That's when the trouble starts. Forgetting their laying duties, the hens start to copy the women's behavior—until the desperate ladies hatch a plan to get what they need. Fun!

Building on Nature: The Life of Antoni Gaudi (Spain)
Rachel Rodriguez; illustrated by Julie Paschkis

Young Antoni loves nature—he notices the details of the landscape that others miss. When he grows up, Antoni studies to become a Spanish architect, weaving the details of nature into his work and changing the rules of architecture at the same time.

EUROPEAN BOOKS FOR AGES 6-8

The Yellow Star: The Legend of King Christian X of Denmark (Denmark)
Carmen Agra Deedy; illustrated by Henri Sorensen

This retelling of a legend describes how the king of Denmark manages to keep his country united during the troubled times of World War II. It specifically showcases the king's courage under pressure. *Note: While this book is clearly aimed at young listeners, it mentions aspects of war that parents might want to preview first.*

This Is London (England) | Miroslav Sasek

From Westminster Abbey to Buckingham Palace, with plenty in between, come meet the faces and see the sights of London! This is one installment from a charming book collection first published in the 1960s. Newer editions make note of any updates in the city or country since the title's initial debut. The nostalgic illustrations appeal to young children, but some of the historical information will likely interest the 8–10 age range more. If your kids enjoy it (and I think they will!), take time to find the others in Sasek's European tour:

- This Is Edinburgh
- This Is Ireland
- This Is Munich
- This Is Paris
- This Is Rome
- This Is Venice

Anatole (France)
Eve Titus; illustrated by Paul Galdone—Caldecott Honor

There couldn't be a happier mouse in all of France—until the night Anatole discovers what humans think of his kind. Determined to change the stereotypes, he devises a strategy to improve the quality of cheese and raise the people's regard for him at the same time. Hilarious!

Charlotte in Giverny (France)
Joan MacPhail Knight; illustrated by Melissa Sweet

Charlotte and her family embark on a voyage to France so her father can paint and learn about Impressionism from the masters. The young girl journals the experience to share with her best friend upon returning to the United States. This first in a series about the fictional Charlotte teaches young readers art history and French culture.

A Giraffe Goes to Paris (France)
Mary Tavener Holmes & John Harris; illustrated by Jon Cannell

Journey along with Belle the giraffe and her caretaker, Atir, as they travel from Egypt to give the animal to the king of France. In 1827, most Parisians had never seen a giraffe, and Belle's arrival in the city causes quite a stir. Based on a fascinating true story.

Katie Meets the Impressionists (France) | James Mayhew

Katie visits an art museum with her grandmother, only to find herself becoming part of the famous paintings. A clever, adventurous introduction to the Impressionists, the story includes works by Monet, Degas, and Renoir. Look for other titles about Katie as well!

The Red Balloon (France) | Albert Lamorisse

Originally an Oscar-winning short film, this story was later adapted into a children's book illustrated with photographs from the movie. Pascal discovers a red balloon that appears to have magical powers. The two become friends, and the balloon comes to the young boy's aid when he needs it most.

Summer Birds: The Butterflies of Maria Merian (Germany)
Margarita Engle; illustrated by Julie Paschkis

During Maria's childhood in seventeenth-century Germany, most people believed insects were evil creatures that developed out of mud. Maria finds insects fascinating, though, and she captures caterpillars to study in secret. She begins to paint the life cycle of these "summer birds," disproving the scientific theories of her time.

GLOBAL PERSPECTIVE

How do you give your children the world in your home?

"I'm half Italian, half Hungarian, and was brought up in Budapest. I live with my family in Belgium, and my husband and I both work for the European Parliament. Keeping our Hungarian roots is a priority. The most important tools for me are books, poetry, music and travel, as well as openness to other people and cultures." Patrizia, Belgium

---

Hanna's Cold Winter (Hungary)
Trish Marx; illustrated by Barbara Knutson

When World War II comes to Budapest, it isn't only the people who begin to starve—the creatures in the zoo suffer as well. In this true story, the city's residents rally together—giving their own straw slippers, doormats, and hats—to save their world-famous hippos. *Note: War/soldiers depicted and mentioned*

The Leprechaun's Gold (Ireland)
Pamela Duncan Edwards; illustrated by Henry Cole

In an old Irish legend, two musicians—kind Old Pat and selfish Young Tom—hope to win the contest for best harpist in the whole country. On the way to the competition, Pat comes to the aid of a leprechaun, who returns the favor with a bit of magic to help the man win the coveted title.

Blockhead: The Life of Fibonacci (Italy)
Joseph D'Agnese; illustrated by John O'Brien

Throughout his childhood, numbers and the quest to make sense of them mesmerize Fibonacci. Misunderstood by those around him, he travels the world and notices how other cultures use numbers. Upon his return to Italy, Fibonacci makes a discovery that puts him in the ranks of the great mathematicians.

Boxes for Katje (Netherlands)
Candace Fleming; illustrated by Stacey Dressen-McQueen

World War II has finally ended and Katje's family has nothing left—until the day the postman delivers a small package from America containing soap, chocolate, and other goods. The relationship that develops helps Katje's entire village survive the hard winter. Based on an inspiring true story!

The Boy Who Held Back the Sea (Netherlands) | Thomas Locker

Gorgeous paintings in the style of the old masters combine with prose to retell this Dutch folktale about a lazy boy who ends up protecting his village. Young Jan has never done a lick of work to help anyone, but when he spots a trickle in the dike, his quick actions save the day.

Katje the Windmill Cat (Netherlands)
Gretchen Woelfle; illustrated by Nicola Bayley

After Katje's owner gets married, the man begins to neglect his pet. So Katje the cat moves into an abandoned windmill so she won't be in the way. When the village floods, Katje courageously proves that she's right where she belongs.

The Fool of the World and the Flying Ship: A Russian Tale (Russia)
Arthur Ransome; illustrated by Uri Shulevitz—Caldecott Medal

The czar announces he will offer his daughter's hand in marriage to any man who brings him a flying ship. Though few believe in him, the Fool of the World takes on the challenge and ends up succeeding.

The Littlest Matryoshka (Russia/U.S.)
Corinne Demas Bliss; illustrated by Kathryn Brown

Matryoshka are Russian "nesting" dolls, with one fitting inside the next. Six matryoshka sisters made in Russia travel across the ocean to a toy store in America, where the smallest one is accidentally swept off the shelf and out the door, beginning an adventurous journey of her own. Will the devoted sisters ever find her again?

Russia ABCs: A Book about the People and Places of Russia (Russia)
Ann Berge; illustrated by Jeff Yesh

This exploration of Russia introduces readers to the people, culture, history, geography, and animals of the country. Learn about Grandfather Frost (who looks an awful lot like Santa but brings gifts on New Year's Day) and the White Nights of St. Petersburg where the sun never sets! *Note: Religious beliefs briefly mentioned*

EUROPEAN BOOKS FOR AGES 8-10

The Wall: Growing Up Behind the Iron Curtain (Czech Republic)
Peter Sis—Caldecott Honor

Peter Sis, children's book author and illustrator, delivers a vivid account of his young life growing up in Czechoslovakia under Soviet rule. The black-and-white illustrations convey the atmosphere of distrust and fear his family lived under—drawing became his way of escape. Also contains fascinating journal excerpts.

> ## GLOBAL PERSPECTIVE
> *How do you give your children the world in your home?*
>
> "We sold most of our belongings, stored the rest, and set out to travel the world indefinitely. I'd dreamed about educating my children that way for years, so we just decided to make it happen. We left last year and are currently in England." Blythe

The Bard of Avon: The Story of William Shakespeare (England)
Diane Stanley & Peter Vennema

Stanley and Vennema introduce readers to a young Shakespeare as he discovers drama for the first time, his years as an actor and then writer, and his work at the Globe Theatre—including the time it burned to the ground during one of his plays. A good starting point for learning about the famous playwright.

Good Queen Bess: The Story of Elizabeth I of England (England)
Diane Stanley & Peter Vennema

Elizabeth refuses to marry and turn her position over to a husband, in spite of her advisors' encouragement. Instead, she steers the country toward security with diplomacy and courage, which endears her to her subjects. An excellent historical overview to Elizabeth's long reign.

The Man Who Made Time Travel (England)
Kathryn Lasky; illustrated by Kevin Hawkes

During the early 1700s, England offered a large financial reward to the person who could develop an accurate method to track longitude while at sea. Many respected scientists attempted theories, but a lowly clockmaker, John Harrison, actually succeeded.

The Butterfly (France) | Patricia Polacco

The Nazis have taken over Monique's village, and war lies heavy in the air. One night, the girl wakes to see another child at the foot of her bed. At first thinking it a ghost, Monique eventually realizes that the Jewish girl has been hiding in her basement. The girls secretly play together in the dark nights until a neighbor discovers them.

The Journey That Saved Curious George:
The True Wartime Escape of Margret and H. A. Rey (France)
Louise W. Borden; illustrated by Allan Drummond

This is Curious George like you've never seen him before! Living as German citizens in France during World War II, Margret and H. A. Rey flee Paris on bicycles as the Nazi army advances. They pack only a few treasured belongings—including their sketches for a picture book featuring one mischievous monkey. An incredible true story.

Marguerite Makes a Book (France)
Bruce Robertson; illustrated by Kathryn Hewitt

A beautiful introduction to the detailed process of bookmaking in medieval times, this is the story of Marguerite, whose father serves the wealthy patrons of Paris as a well-known manuscript illuminator. When she notices her aging father struggling to accomplish his work, Marguerite takes over in order to deliver his commission on time.

Secret Seder (France)
Doreen Rappaport; illustrated by Emily Arnold McCully

Jacques and his Jewish family live in a small village in France, where they pretend to be Catholics during World War II. Even in the midst of tremendous danger, they decide to celebrate the Passover with friends—remembering their history and praying for freedom. *Note: Religious beliefs mentioned*

Shooting at the Stars: The Christmas Truce of 1914 (France)
John Hendrix

In this unbelievable true story, German and British soldiers take Christmas Day off during World War I to exchange gifts and sing carols. They meet in No Man's Land to bury the fallen, later playing a game of football before heading back to their own sides and continuing the war the next day. Thought-provoking.

Luba: The Angel of Bergen-Belsen (Germany)
Michelle R. McCann; illustrated by Ann Marshall

Luba has lost her young son and husband to the concentration camps; she struggles to understand why she has been spared. The answer arrives the night she discovers fifty-four Jewish children abandoned and terrified in the forest near her barracks. At great personal risk, Luba cares for and hides them throughout the long winter.

One Thousand Tracings: Healing the Wounds of World War II (Germany)
Lita Judge

The war has ended, but the suffering has not. An American family begins to gather shoes and other supplies for German survivors, helping them through the first long winter after the war. Includes original photographs and foot tracings.

What's Your Angle, Pythagoras? (Greece)
Julie Ellis; illustrated by Phyllis Hornung

Young Pythagoras is always in the way—curious and adventurous, exploring and trying to figure things out. Though others consider him troublesome, his calculations go on to solve many community problems. A fictionalized account of his famous mathematical theorem's discovery.

The Irish Cinderlad (Ireland)
Shirley Climo; illustrated by Loretta Krupinski

A twist on the popular fairy tale, this is the story of Becan—a boy with a cruel stepmother and stepsisters. A magical bull takes the place of the fairy godmother, and a princess searches for the owner of the large boot left behind after her rescue from a dragon!

Galileo's Leaning Tower Experiment (Italy)
Wendy Macdonald; illustrated by Paolo Rui

Massimo, a young farm boy, has an unexpected encounter with Galileo that changes his life in this fictionalized story of the famous scientist's work. Together the two test and disprove one of Aristotle's theories by dropping different objects, which fall at the same rate, from the Leaning Tower of Pisa.

Leonardo: Beautiful Dreamer (Italy) | Robert Byrd

Introduce your children to sides of this renowned artist they may not have encountered before, including his talent as a musician, architect, and engineer. This tribute to da Vinci's genius highlights his journals and futuristic designs—chock-full of information for interested readers.

Leonardo's Horse (Italy) | Jean Fritz; illustrated by Hudson Talbott

A story of Leonardo da Vinci you might never have come across, this book describes the artist's dream to sculpt a massive bronze horse. He dies before the vision is realized, but centuries later an American takes up the challenge of completing the horse and offers it as a gift to the people of Italy.

Michelangelo (Italy) | Diane Stanley

Sculpting David catapulted Michelangelo to the forefront of Renaissance art, but what was his life like before he achieved fame? In this read, find out about the artist's upbringing, how he got his start, his joys and frustrations, and his later years. *Note: One illustration shows the artist cutting open a human cadaver to study anatomy.*

Starry Messenger: Galileo Galilei (Italy) | Peter Sis

These pages emphasize Galileo's courage, his belief that Earth was not the center of the universe and his defense of that position even in the face of exile. I was also struck by the clear love of learning that kept him questioning and making new discoveries—his quotes in the sidebars fascinated me!

A Day on Skates: The Story of a Dutch Picnic (Netherlands)
Hilda van Stockum—Newbery Honor

Holland comes alive in this sweet story and its nostalgic illustrations, originally published in 1934. Nine-year-old twins Evert and Afke go with their class and teacher for a winter ice-skating picnic, which kicks off a string of childlike adventures.

The Cats in Krasinski Square (Poland)
Karen Hesse; illustrated by Wendy Watson

Follow a young girl in Warsaw during World War II, when Polish Jews must live in a guarded section of the city. Having escaped the ghetto themselves, the girl and her sister work with others to get food and supplies to those in need—even if it means outwitting the Gestapo to do so.

The Champion of Children: The Story of Janusz Korczak (Poland)
Tomek Bogacki

Even as a young boy in Warsaw, Janusz Korczak imagines a better world for kids in need. He never loses sight of this mission—eventually becoming a doctor and advocacy writer as well as designing an orphanage for young Jews. As the Nazis draw closer, Korczak refuses to abandon "his" children—accompanying them to the very end. Amazing.

Peter the Great (Russia) | Diane Stanley

Young Peter, crowned tsar at age ten, grows up with extravagance and immense power. But as he gets older, Peter realizes that what he longs for most is to lead Russia into the modern era of the eighteenth century. So he leaves the country in disguise to learn what he can from other countries, and he returns with a host of innovative ideas.

GLOBAL PERSPECTIVE

How do you give your children the world in your home?

"My husband and I both have graduate degrees in international affairs, have traveled quite a bit, and speak various languages. Our children are still quite young (four, two, and six months), so we are starting to read picture books from different countries, and we have a globe, maps, and flags around our home for them to look at. They enjoy looking through a picture dictionary in French (my second language), and though we don't purposely try to 'teach' them any other languages, we have rich discussions about language and words, where they come from and how they are interconnected." Heather, Washington State

Pictures at an Exhibition (Russia)
Anna Harwell Celenza; illustrated by JoAnn Kitchel

When a Russian composer, Modest Mussorgsky, loses one of his best friends unexpectedly, he plunges into despair without any desire to continue his music. Then he attends an exhibition of his deceased friend's artwork, and a stirring in his soul leads him to create a composition in honor of his friend.

EUROPEAN BOOKS FOR AGES 10–12

The Star of Kazan (Austria) | Eva Ibbotson

Each year, Annika celebrates her "Found Day," when the servants discovered her abandoned in a nearby church. The cook and housemaid raise the girl themselves until the day Annika has always imagined arrives: her mother, a noble and wealthy woman, shows up. But Annika's new life isn't all it seems, and the young girl must escape before it's too late. Takes place in pre-WWI Vienna.

Hana's Suitcase (Czech Republic) | Karen Levine

Based on a radio documentary, this book describes what happens when a suitcase with the name Hana Brady on it arrives at the Tokyo Children's Holocaust Education Center. The director of the museum sets out to learn more and ends up discovering the personal story of Hana Brady, a Jewish girl living in a small Czech town during the Nazi invasion.

The Crow-Girl (Denmark) | Bodil Bredsdorff

The Crow-Girl lives peacefully with her grandmother on the outskirts of a tiny Danish village. Sensing she's nearing her end, the old woman begins passing on the wisdom she believes her granddaughter needs. Soon the young girl must make a new life for herself and test out the advice she's received. The first in a series.

Number the Stars (Denmark) | Lois Lowry—Newbery Medal

Ten-year-olds Annemarie and Ellen have been best friends for as long as they can remember. But now they're sisters too. At least they're pretending to be, since Nazi officers are on every corner, coming to round up Jews like Ellen and her family. Inspire your kids with this real-life effort by courageous Danes to smuggle their Jewish countrymen to safety in Sweden before it's too late. An exciting read-aloud!

Archie's War (England) | Marcia Williams

Experience World War I through the eyes of Archie Albright, a fictional British boy who loves comics and compiles a "scrapbook" to remember the war years. The author presents plenty of historical information through the eyes of this resilient tween.

The Cheshire Cheese Cat: A Dickens of a Tale (England)
Carmen Agra Deedy & Randall Wright

Skilley the cat just got his big break. He's taken a position as the official mouser at Ye Olde Cheshire Cheese—the London inn that serves as a hangout for Charles Dickens and other writers. Throw in a literate mouse named Pip, an author struggling with a new novel, and an appearance by Queen Victoria and you have a historical novel waiting to be enjoyed.

Good Masters! Sweet Ladies! Voices from a Medieval Village (England)
Laura Amy Schlitz; illustrated by Robert Byrd—Newbery Medal

Time-travel back to the year 1255 and meet over twenty individuals who live in a medieval village. From the plowboy to the doctor's son, the lord's daughter to the beggar, you'll gain perspective on their lives through the short vignettes each character delivers.

War Horse (England/France/Germany) | Michael Morpurgo

Joey, an English farm horse, once belonged to thirteen-year-old Albert. But at the start of World War I, Albert's father sold him to the army. Now the dangers of battle constantly surround the horse as he transports artillery and wounded soldiers, wondering if he'll ever see Albert again. A moving story with a unique viewpoint of war.

Black Radishes (France) | Susan Lynn Meyer

Gustave's parents no longer think Paris is safe for Jews, so they move to a small country village. Soon the Nazi army occupies Paris, and other areas of the nation also sense impending danger. With the help of the French Resistance, eleven-year-old Gustave comes up with a plan to get his family to America—if they don't get captured first.

The Grand Mosque of Paris: A Story of How Muslims Rescued Jews During the Holocaust (France)
Karen Gray Ruelle & Deborah Durland DeSaix

During World War II, many Jews in Paris took shelter at an unexpected location: the city's mosque. This book chronicles the incredible true story of Muslims who willingly put their own lives at risk to save those of another faith. *Note: Muslim and Jewish beliefs mentioned*

The Invention of Hugo Cabret (France)
Brian Selznick—Caldecott Medal

This half-graphic, half-written novel introduces readers to twelve-year-old Hugo Cabret, an orphan living in a Parisian train station. His life mission? Day-to-day survival—and the repair of a broken mechanical man he believes holds a meaningful secret. When Hugo's life intersects with the lives of a toy shop owner and his goddaughter, Hugo accepts the girl's help to solve his mystery.

Joan of Arc (France) | Demi

In this touching biography, Joan of Arc bravely answers God's call to lead her country against invaders. The inspiring illustrations reflect the stained glass vignettes popular in the fifteenth century. If you enjoy Demi's style, look for her other titles about historic figures. *Note: Christian beliefs mentioned*

Something Out of Nothing: Marie Curie and Radium (France)
Carla Killough McClafferty

This title reveals both the well-known and the more obscure details about this Nobel Prize winner, including Marie's poor childhood, her keen desire to learn, and her remarkable world-changing discovery. The author also gives voice to the controversies that marked the scientist's life and how her death resulted from her life's work.

Truce: The Day the Soldiers Stopped Fighting (France) | Jim Murphy

Truce doesn't shy away from the horrors of war, but it also shows hope in the midst of suffering. On Christmas Day 1914, soldiers on both sides of the trenches declare a temporary truce with the enemy. Meeting in No Man's Land, the men celebrate together. Includes photographs of the actual event.

Twenty and Ten (France) | Claire Huchet Bishop

The kids love to play "escape from the enemy" in the schoolyard, but an opportunity arises that takes their game to an unimagined level. Can twenty school children successfully keep ten Jewish youngsters hidden from the Nazis? With the help of Sister Gabriel, their teacher, that's what they determine to do. *Note: Christian and Jewish beliefs mentioned*

GLOBAL PERSPECTIVE

How do you give your children the world in your home?

"We had the opportunity when our son was in Kindergarten to take a job in Germany. The two years we were supposed to be there turned into six. We had some wonderful German neighbors and traveled all over the European Union. One of our favorite trips was nine days to Turkey, where we traveled from Istanbul to Cappadocia to Pammakule to Side. We taught our son to try the local cuisine. Most of the meals provided were very different, but I was so proud of him for trying everything. We had some great experiences and some not-so-great, but I wouldn't trade a thing for the memories!" Jennifer, Kentucky

After the Train (Germany) | Gloria Whelan

Though the war ended ten years ago, Peter's teachers won't let any of the students forget what happened to the Jews in their country. He doesn't understand why they can't move on. But everything changes the day Peter discovers a letter revealing that he is actually Jewish.

Candy Bomber: The Story of the Berlin Airlift's "Chocolate Pilot" (Germany) | Michael O. Tunnell

Lieutenant Gail Halvorsen, a pilot for the U.S. Air Force, has no idea that offering a few German kids a stick of gum will change his life. Seeing their eager response, Halvorsen decides to do a candy and chocolate drop from his aircraft. The project grows with publicity, and Halvorsen endears himself to an entire generation of post-WWII kids.

When Hitler Stole Pink Rabbit (Germany/Switzerland/France) | Judith Kerr

Nine-year-old Anna doesn't understand why her family has to leave Germany. She knows the situation must be serious, though, when she wakes one morning to find her father has disappeared. Alongside her brother and mother, Anna begins life as a war refugee and leaves behind her prized possessions—including her special pink rabbit. This novel, based on the author's life, was one of our family's first World War II read-alouds.

Nory Ryan's Song (Ireland) | Patricia Reilly Giff

Nory Ryan's Song gives readers a glimpse into the devastating Irish Potato Famine. As a member of a poor farming family who pays rent to a cruel English lord, twelve-year-old Nory knows hunger well. But when she discovers their entire potato crop ruined, Nory learns the difference between hunger and starvation. Now she must help her family stay together . . . and survive.

Roman Diary: The Journal of Iliona of Mytilini: Captured and Sold As a Slave in Rome, AD 107 (Italy)
Richard Platt; illustrated by David Parkins

Iliona, a fictionalized Greek noble girl, becomes a slave of the Roman Empire when pirates overtake the ship she's traveling on. Slowly she adjusts to her new position in life, while continuing to dream of freedom. The book doesn't shy away from the darker sides of her experience, yet it doesn't go into excessive detail either.

Eli Remembers (Lithuania)
Ruth Vander Zee, Marian Sneider; illustrated by Bill Farnsworth

Eli watches his family light the candles during Rosh Hashanah, never understanding why a deep sadness tinges their celebrations each year. He finds out much later, when he travels to Lithuania and his relatives share the tragic events that occurred during the Holocaust. *Note: Contains a somewhat graphic description of Holocaust deaths*

Snow Treasure (Norway) | Marie McSwigan

It's 1940 and the residents of a small Norwegian village have lost their freedom but not their power. They develop a daring plan to smuggle the gold out of their banks before the Nazis can use it. Knowing adults could never pull off the heist, they enlist the help of the village children, who sneak the gold down to the fjord in their sleds. Exciting!

Breaking Stalin's Nose (Russia) | Eugene Yelchin—Newbery Honor

Growing up during Stalin's reign, ten-year-old Sasha is on the cusp of achieving a childhood dream: joining the Young Pioneers. Like his father, a member of the secret police, the boy considers himself a proud Communist. But the night before his Pioneer rally, Sasha's father is arrested and the boy begins to question his beliefs.

A Faraway Island (Sweden) | Annika Thor

Twelve-year-old Stephie's and eight-year-old Nellie's parents hope to escape the Nazis and move to the United States. While they secure visas, they send their two Jewish daughters to safety in Sweden. The sisters live in different foster families and face hard times alone, wondering if they will ever see their loved ones again. The first in a series.

The Unfinished Angel (Switzerland) | Sharon Creech

Zola just moved to a tiny Swiss village with her father, who is tired of American "incivility" and wants to start a more peaceful life. The young girl doesn't expect to meet a quirky angel in her new home, but after their first encounter, the two team up for a series of minor miracles—including the rescue of several homeless orphans.

CHAPTER 8

THE WEAVING OF A DREAM: ASIA

Countries/regions included in this chapter: Bangladesh, Cambodia, China, India, Indonesia, Japan, Korea, Mongolia, Philippines, Thailand, Tibet, Vietnam

It's hard for me to imagine a more idyllic place for children to heal from the trauma of trafficking than Love146's beautiful safehome in the Philippine countryside. A therapy treehouse invites the girls who live there to learn how to play again. Art and music allow them to express both their pain and their rekindled dreams for the future, while a farm and vegetable garden let them experience nature's healing.

When Trishna and I had the chance to visit in 2013, the girls proudly gave us a tour. Upon reaching their schoolroom, we noticed just one thing missing: a well-stocked library of stories. I put out a call on my blog and before our family headed back to the States, my incredible community of generous readers had donated over ten thousand dollars—enough not only to stock the bookshelves, but also to pay for an entire year of the girls' education!

Sharing books with others is one of my greatest joys. I hope you feel the same way after poring through this list.

ASIAN BOOKS FOR AGES 4–6

GLOBAL PERSPECTIVE

How do you give your children the world in your home?

"We have a map and globe that we refer to when we come across different countries in the books we read or the shows we watch. I deliberately look for children's books on different cultures when we are at thrift stores. Sometimes when the kids have a question about a certain place, we turn to the internet for resources. I also encourage them to choose a place on our globe that we can pray for during our morning prayer time. Someday we would love to worldschool! We plan to start small first though, and travel around the Philippines and Southeast Asia."
Tina, Philippines

Dim Sum for Everyone! (China) | Grace Lin

A family goes to a dim sum restaurant and selects their favorite Chinese foods from the trolleys passing by. They share and sample each one. Features a note at the end of the book detailing the history of dim sum.

The Empty Pot (China) | Demi

The emperor announces that the child who produces the most beautiful flower will become his successor. Ping has a green thumb, but nothing he does for his seed helps it grow. Discouraged but honest, he appears before the emperor with his empty pot, only to receive the shock of his young life. I love this story!

Ling & Ting: Not Exactly the Same! (China) | Grace Lin

Ling and Ting may look alike, but these identical twin girls are far from the same! Whether making dumplings, using chopsticks, or getting haircuts, Ling always does what's expected, while Ting adds in a little mischief to keep life interesting. A laugh-inducing read-aloud for your littles, or a fun early reader for your six- to eight-year-olds.

Round Is a Mooncake: A Book of Shapes (China/U.S.)
Roseanne Thong; illustrated by Grace Lin

In short poems paired with brightly colored drawings, a young girl examines the shapes around her home and neighborhood. Through her eyes, readers get to know objects that relate to her Chinese heritage—like round mooncakes, a rectangle cricket box, and square dim sum.

Two of Everything (China) | Lily Toy Hong
The adventure begins when Mr. Haktak finds a brass pot in his garden. He places his purse inside as he carries it home. Later, his wife pulls out not one but two purses. The couple joyfully realizes it's a magic pot and believes their troubles are over. All goes well until the day when Mrs. Haktak herself falls inside!

The Monkey and the Crocodile: A Jataka Tale from India (India)
Paul Galdone

A hungry crocodile craves the taste of monkey, but how can he catch one when they never come near the water? He comes up with a clever strategy, but it turns out he's not the only smart animal in the jungle.

Same, Same but Different (India) | Jenny Sue Kostecki-Shaw
Elliot from America and Kailash from India become "picture pals" and eventually best friends—comparing their houses, families, pets, and schools as they write and send drawings to each other. Their discovery? That most things in their lives are the same with just a little that's different. Fun and sweet!

The Story of Little Babaji (India)
Helen Bannerman; illustrated by Fred Marcellino

Little Babaji's parents have given him clothes, shoes, and a beautiful green umbrella. But when tigers threaten the boy in the jungle, Little Babaji must offer them the new garments to save his own life. Can he trick the animals and get his things back?

The Paper Crane (Japan) | Molly Bang
In this folktale, a busy restaurant owner receives a rude awakening when a newly constructed highway detours most of his customers. One night a poor man enters, asking for a meal. He pays for his food with a magical paper crane that brings prosperity—and crowds—back to the restaurant.

Today and Today (Japan)
Kobayashi Issa; illustrated by G. Brian Karas

This haiku collection by a well-known Japanese poet proceeds through each of the four seasons, highlighting typical scenes of family life. A charming introduction to haiku for children.

Bee-bim Bop! (Korea) | Linda Sue Park; illustrated by Ho Baek Lee

A hungry daughter goes with her mother to the market and home again, eagerly awaiting the making of her favorite dish, bee-bim bop. This book features rhyming text and a recipe to try out.

Filipino Friends (Philippines)
Liana Romulo; illustrated by Corazon Dandan-Albano

Sam, a Filipino-American child, visits the Philippines for the first time and shares with young readers the differences in culture he notices. Each page has only a few words but incorporates sidebars with more detail, making this a fitting read for ages 6–8 as well.

Hush! A Thai Lullaby (Thailand)
Minfong Ho & Holly Meade—Caldecott Honor

Mama determines to quiet all the animal noises in her remote village that might wake the baby: the mosquito, the lizard, the water buffalo, the elephant. The animals settle down and the mama finally falls asleep—but guess who is stirring now?

ASIAN BOOKS FOR AGES 6-8

Silent Lotus (Cambodia) | Jeanne M. Lee

Young Lotus cannot hear or speak. Hoping to find help for their daughter, her parents take her to the nearest temple. When Lotus sees the temple dancers, she begins to imitate them. Her movements are so graceful that the king and queen grant her a favored position in the court. *Note: Buddhist beliefs mentioned*

Chinese and English Nursery Rhymes: Share and Sing in Two Languages
(China) | Faye-Lynn Wu; illustrated by Kieren Dutcher

This book shares familiar nursery rhymes in both English and Chinese, organized by themes like outside, inside, play, and night. It incorporates plenty of appealing illustrations as well as a CD to learn correct pronunciation.

Count Your Way Through China (China)
Jim Haskins; illustrated by Dennis Hockerman

Chinese numbers one through ten are paired with historical and cultural details on these pages—including animals, instruments, climate, art, and more.

GLOBAL PERSPECTIVE

How do you give your children the world in your home?

"We have a large world map and are always checking it when we order meals or read books. My husband and I went to Rome on our honeymoon, so I shared with my daughter stories from our trip. We saw an exhibit on China recently that opened up more global conversations. We make it part of everyday learning and play." Jen, Missouri

Crouching Tiger (China/U.S.)
Ying Chang Compestine; illustrated by Yan Nascimbene

The tai chi Grandpa calmly rehearses isn't nearly as interesting as the kung fu moves his grandson Vinson hopes to learn. After a scary close call, though, Vinson changes his mind and begins to practice with Grandpa, earning the boy a role in the Chinese New Year parade.

Daisy Comes Home (China) | Jan Brett

Mei Mei proudly takes care of the six happiest hens in China, but the smallest hen, Daisy, gets picked on by the others. She decides to escape from the bullying hens for the night and makes her bed in a basket near the river. When she wakes, Daisy finds herself floating in the water alone! How will she make it back home?

The Emperor and the Kite (China) | Jane Yolen

Djeow, whose name means "tiny," is the youngest and often overlooked daughter of the emperor. Her brothers and sisters steal their father's attention—until the day an enemy locks the emperor in a tower. Only Djeow and her kite hold the key to his freedom!

The Five Chinese Brothers (China)
Claire Huchet Bishop; illustrated by Kurt Wiese

The five Chinese brothers each have a unique, extraordinary power. In this traditional folktale, they must use their abilities to rescue and save the oldest brother from certain death.

Grandfather Counts (China/U.S.)
Andrea Cheng; illustrated by Ange Zhang

When Gong Gong (Grandfather) first arrives, the adjustment is hard for Helen. She has to move out of her bedroom and can't communicate with him. But the pair bond through their mutual fascination with the train that passes behind the house, and soon they teach each other to count and write their names in Chinese and English.

Grandfather Tang's Story (China)
Ann Tompert; illustrated by Robert Andrew Parker

Grandfather Tang uses tangrams to tell his granddaughter about two fox fairies that continue to change their shape until they must work together to escape danger. Clever!

Lon Po Po: A Red-Riding Hood Story from China (China)
Ed Young—Caldecott Medal

Mother leaves her three daughters alone to go visit Grandmother for her birthday. The wolf, Lon Po Po, creeps to their home at night in disguise. Can the girls outwit him and save themselves? *Note: Some illustrations may frighten sensitive readers.*

Look What Came from China! (China) | Miles Harvey

This title covers the inventions, foods, tools, musical instruments, and more that originated in China. It includes recipes, a helpful glossary, and a pronunciation guide as well.

Ming Lo Moves the Mountain (China) | Arnold Lobel

Ming Lo and his wife live beside a mountain—a mountain that blocks the sun, drops rocks on their home, and brings rain their way. Ming Lo's frustrated wife issues an order to her husband—he must move that mountain! Another charming title by the author of the Frog and Toad Series.

The Pet Dragon: A Story about Adventure, Friendship, and Chinese Characters (China) | Christoph Niemann

This clever book teaches thirty-three Chinese characters through the story of Lin and her pet dragon. When Lin and the dragon break a precious vase, her father insists she keep the pet in a cage. The dragon escapes and the adventure begins as Lin sets out to find her friend.

Ruby's Wish (China) | Shirin Yim; illustrated by Sophie Blackall

Ruby isn't like most of the girls in her large family. She wears red, the color of celebration, each and every day. And while the others dream of getting married, Ruby hopes to attend university. Will it ever happen? Based on an inspiring true story.

The Seeing Stick (China) | Jane Yolen; illustrated by Daniela Terrazzini

Hwei Min, the only daughter of the emperor, has been blind since birth. Her rich father promises lavish rewards to anyone who can cure her, but it's no use. One day a mysterious visitor with a magical "seeing stick" helps Hwei Min in an unexpected, and life-changing, way.

The Seven Chinese Sisters (China)
Kathy Tucker; illustrated by Grace Lin

Each of the seven Chinese sisters has a special talent and magical power, but the baby has yet to discover hers. When a dragon snatches her, the others must snap into action and whisk the little girl back to safety.

Sparrow Girl (China) | Sara Pennypacker

Ming-Li and her village have been ordered to fight and kill an enemy—the sparrows blamed for eating the community's grain. The girl and her older brother, upset by the plan, rescue and hide seven of the birds. Later the farmers discover that the sparrows were actually helping the village and the hidden birds save the day.

The Story about Ping (China)
Marjorie Flack; illustrated by Kurt Wiese

Ping is a duck who lives with his family on a Yangtze riverboat. The ducks spend their days looking for food until the master calls them each night, when they return and board the boat. One day Ping misses the call and spends his night exploring instead.

Tikki Tikki Tembo (China) | Arlene Mosel; illustrated by Blair Lent

According to a Chinese folktale, years ago parents gave their firstborn sons long names as a sign of honor. But when firstborn Tikki tikki tembo-no sa rembo-chari bari ruchi-pip peri pembo and his younger brother Chang fall into a well, the eldest nearly drowns because it takes so long to call him. Old Man with a Ladder comes to the rescue, and the boys change history in the process.

I Is for India (India) | Prodeepta Das

This alphabetical introduction to India offers a photographic overview of customs, language, and culture. When the kids were younger, we read this title each year on Trishna's India Day. *Note: Religious beliefs mentioned*

GLOBAL PERSPECTIVE
How do you give your children the world in your home?

"We took our five kids to live in a remote village in India on the Nepal border in an orphanage for fourteen months. It changed our family and our children. Not all people can do this, but we have a new family that consists of 160 people we love." Dawna

Monsoon (India) | Uma Krishnaswami; illustrated by Jamel Akib

The sights and sounds of a busy northern India street star on these pages: traffic, market stalls, life at home. A young girl, her family, and the whole town watch the sky, waiting for the much-needed monsoon rains to begin. She shares her concern that maybe they won't come at all, but finally the sky pours forth and the city rejoices!

The Bicycle Man (Japan) | Allen Say

Soon after the end of World War II, the children in a Japanese village arrive at school ready to compete in their "sports day." When two American soldiers show up unexpectedly, they amaze the students with their bicycle tricks and take home a special prize.

Crow Boy (Japan) | Taro Yahima—Caldecott Honor

Chibi's classmates exclude him because of his differences: he's small, quiet, and afraid of the others. Then a new teacher arrives who helps the class appreciate Chibi's talents. Such an important message—the power of one mentor to influence a child's life!

The Funny Little Woman (Japan)
Arlene Mosel & Blair Lent—Caldecott Medal

The funny little woman lives all alone, busy with her work as a dumpling maker. One day when a dumpling falls through a crack in her floor, she chases it—only to find herself in a magical world surrounded by evil creatures. Can she escape?

Grandfather's Journey (Japan) | Allen Say—Caldecott Medal

A young man leaves Japan for the new world of America, then returns to marry his childhood sweetheart. They come back to the States to start their family, but he continues to be torn by his love for both countries. When in one, he longs for the other.

Hachiko: The True Story of a Loyal Dog (Japan)
Pamela S. Turner; illustrated by Yan Nascimbene

Hachiko walks with his master to Shibuya train station every day and waits for him to return in the afternoon. One sad day, however, his master never comes home. The faithful dog keeps up his vigil for years—becoming a national symbol of love and loyalty.

How My Parents Learned to Eat (Japan)
Ina R. Friedman; illustrated by Allen Say

An American sailor stationed overseas falls in love with a Japanese woman. He doesn't know how to use chopsticks, and she doesn't know how to use a knife and fork. This cross-cultural love story made my kids smile.

Kamishibai Man (Japan) | Allen Say

The Kamishibai man retired long ago, but he decides to take his paper theater, drawings, and homemade candy on the streets one last time. While waiting for kids to arrive, he remembers the old days—when children crowded around him instead of the television. Before the day's end, the man finds out that he impacted the community more than he could have imagined. A good read for TV-free week!

The Magic Fan (Japan) | Keith Baker

Yoshi builds everything in the village—houses, fences, tables, and more. When he runs out of possibilities, a fan floating in the sea gives him new ones—including the idea to build a bridge. The villagers disapprove—until the day when Yoshi's bridge saves their lives.

A Pair of Red Clogs (Japan)
Masako Matsuno; illustrated by Kazue Mizumura

Mako loves the red clogs her mother gave her, but she accidentally cracks them while playing a game. Her desire for a new pair tempts her to lie. Told from the perspective of a grandmother looking back on her own childhood pair of shoes.

Tea with Milk (Japan) | Allen Say

May grows up in America and struggles with severe culture shock when her parents decide to take the family back to Japan permanently. Not wanting to be paired off in marriage against her will, she travels to Osaka to find work, where she meets and falls in love with Joseph, a young man also adjusting to a new home.

The Way We Do It in Japan (Japan)
Geneva Cobb Iijima; illustrated by Paige Billin-Frye

Come along with Gregory as he moves with his mother and father from the United States to Japan. Throughout his journey and transition, the boy learns about the foods, furniture, language, customs, and schooling in his new country.

Dear Juno (Korea)
Soyung Pak; illustrated by Susan Kathleen Hartung

Juno, who lives in the United States, misses his grandmother, who's still in Korea. But the pair finds a special way to communicate, in spite of the fact that Juno can't read Korean and his grandmother can't read English. Using drawings, photos, and nature, they discuss their lives with each other—and in the end Juno happily discovers that Grandmother is on her way!

The Firekeeper's Son (Korea)
Linda Sue Park; illustrated by Julie Downing

Sang-hee's father lights a fire each night on the top of his assigned mountain—a signal to the king that all is well in the land. Yet one evening a sudden injury prevents him from doing his work and Sang-hee must take over. Can the boy start the fire before the king sends out soldiers? Set in the early 1800s, this is one for your adventure lovers!

K Is for Korea (Korea)
Hyechong Cheung; illustrated by Prodeepta Das

This title uses colorful photographs combined with the alphabet to introduce young readers to aspects of Korean life and culture. *Note: Religious beliefs mentioned*

Horse Song: The Naadam of Mongolia (Mongolia)
Ted & Betsy Lewin

The authors travel to Mongolia to observe the well-known Naadam summer horse race. Along the way, they describe their trip, the fourteen-mile race, and Mongolian culture. The couple visits nine-year-old Tamir, one of the young horse jockeys, as he and his family prepare for the competition they hope he will win.

Grandfather's Dream (Vietnam) | Holly Keller

Grandfather remembers when cranes, a symbol of luck for the community, filled the sky. After the war, however, the birds vanished. The younger generation believes that the land set aside for cranes would be put to better use growing rice. But Grandfather has a dream—and eventually, it comes true.

GLOBAL PERSPECTIVE

How do you give your children the world in your home?

"Our two oldest children write back and forth with girls their same age who live in Uganda. Last year, I finished training as a midwife in the Philippines and came back home with countless stories about the children and families that I met. Our children spent a few months putting together gifts and packages to send to our new friends living there. I look forward to the day when my whole family can hop on a plane and visit." Sarah, Virginia

The Lotus Seed (Vietnam)
Sherry Garland; illustrated by Tatsuro Kiuchi

A young girl wants to remember the emperor after he loses his throne, so she takes a lotus seed from the Imperial garden. She keeps it during her life—through the dangers of war, as she flees her country by boat, and while starting over in a foreign land. Years later, the lotus seed connects her entire family to their culture and heritage. *Note: Contains descriptions of war*

ASIAN BOOKS FOR AGES 8–10

Rickshaw Girl (Bangladesh) | Mitali Perkins
Ten-year-old Naima paints the village's most beautiful traditional patterns, but she wishes she could earn money like a boy. Her father works long hours driving a rickshaw, and in an attempt to help him, Naima accidentally crashes it—leaving the family worse off than before. In the end, her talent as a painter opens the door to a job and also changes her family's beliefs about girls.

Chee-Lin: A Giraffe's Journey (China) | James Rumford
Beginning in Africa, journeying to India, and ending in China, this picture book tells the story of Chee-Lin: a giraffe who becomes a Chinese symbol of luck and prosperity. Based on a true account, it takes place in the early 1400s when China sent ships to explore the world and bring back its treasures.

The Emperor's Silent Army: Terracotta Warriors of Ancient China (China) | Jane O'Connor

In 1974, three farmers uncovered a head made out of pottery while digging a well. Archeologists soon found a remarkable discovery—an entire army of thousands of terracotta soldiers, created by order of the first Emperor of China. Fascinating photographs!

The Moon Lady (China) | Amy Tan; illustrated by Gretchen Schields

Nai-nai overhears her grandchildren wishing for fun on a boring, rainy day. She tells them her own childhood story about meeting the moon lady, who grants secret desires, at a Chinese festival. There she learned that the best wishes are those you can make come true by yourself.

The Silk Route: 7,000 Miles of History (China)
John S. Major; illustrated by Stephen Fieser

This title traces the journey of valuable silk in ancient times—beginning in China and following a seven-thousand-mile route to Europe. Venturing through deserts, storms, heat, and bandits, travelers risked their lives to arrive with the goods at their destination.

The Weaving of a Dream (China) | Marilee Heyer

An old widow, with three sons to support, ventures to the market to trade her weavings for rice. But when she arrives, she becomes obsessed with a painting of a palace and buys it instead. She spends the next three years copying the artwork into an intricate brocade, but it isn't until the wind snatches it away that the family's adventure truly starts. *Note: Religious beliefs mentioned*

The Year of the Panda (China)
Miriam Schlein; illustrated by Kam Mak

Lu Yi and his father rescue a baby panda and nurse it back to health. Soon they discover that the pandas' food supply has run out, and the animals will die if more bamboo isn't grown. The government offers money to any farmers, including Lu Yi's father, who will relocate so their land can be used to save future generations of pandas.

Yeh-Shen: A Cinderella Story from China (China) | Ai-Ling Louie

It's festival time, and poor Yeh-Shen must spend all her days cooking and cleaning for her stepmother and stepsister. A familiar tale of magic and a tiny golden slipper follows—bringing Yeh-Shen both justice and the love of the king. This Chinese version of Cinderella is a thousand years older than its Western counterpart.

Grandfather Gandhi (India)
Arun Gandhi & Bethany Hegedus; illustrated by Evan Turk

Written by Gandhi's grandson, this book describes the boy's secret worry that he might not live up to the Gandhi family name. When a bully makes him angry, he runs to Grandfather Gandhi, who reminds him that anger isn't the problem—it's what you do with it that matters. A powerful read for any child who struggles with a temper! *Note: Religious beliefs briefly mentioned*

Indian Tales (India) | Shenaaz Nanji: illustrated by Christopher Corr

This colorful anthology, produced by Barefoot Books, provides an introduction to India's well-known folktales. Each story comes from a different region of the country and includes cultural notes specific to the area. The eight adventurous tales feature characters including robbers, traditional spirits, gods and goddesses, and brave heroes. *Note: Religious beliefs mentioned*

Cycle of Rice, Cycle of Life (Indonesia) | Jan Reynolds

This book describes in detail the process of rice farming on the island of Bali. Farmers live in tune with the earth's rhythms—rotating crops and sharing water with neighbors in a holistic manner that flows from their spiritual and social beliefs. The success of their system has made Bali one of the world's leading producers of rice. *Note: Religious beliefs mentioned*

The Boy of the Three-Year Nap (Japan)
Dianne Snyder—Caldecott Honor

Taro never works, much to the dismay of his poor, widowed mother. But when he wants to marry the daughter of a rich merchant, his mother comes up with a cunning plan to climb out of poverty and change her son's lazy ways at the same time.

Hachiko Waits (Japan)
Lesléa Newman; illustrated by Machiyo Kodaira

Every morning faithful dog Hachiko accompanies his master to the train station. Every afternoon he waits patiently until his owner returns. One day, however, no master comes home. Undaunted in his devotion, the dog continues to wait—for ten years! This version of Hachiko's true story goes into more detail about death, both of a person and a beloved pet, making it a better fit for slightly older readers than the title listed in the 6–8 section.

GLOBAL PERSPECTIVE

How do you give your children the world in your home?

"As a military family, we live on base and we're surrounded by people from everywhere. Some of our closest friends are from Guam, and we've had neighbors from Germany and all over the U.S. My kids have an 'array' of friends and are open to trying new foods and learning other languages. When we meet someone, we like to find out where they're from and look up information about their home. We've exposed my kids to a diversity that I never had growing up, and I love that." Kelley, Colorado

---

Manjiro: The Boy Who Risked His Life for Two Countries (Japan)
Emily Arnold McCully

Fourteen-year-old Manjiro's real-life adventure begins when his fishing boat shipwrecks on a deserted island in 1841. Eventually rescued by an American whaling ship, Manjiro, with his desire to learn, impresses the captain, who invites the boy to America. Years later, Manjiro decides to return to Japan. He travels home with a big task ahead of him—convincing the country to let him in when they have been closed to the outside world for over 250 years.

The Perfect Sword (Japan) | Scott Goto

Together with his master, apprentice Michio creates the perfect sword. The pair must then find the right owner for it. It must not go to the strongest, the fiercest, or the best—but to the one most worthy. They deny many likely candidates until they stumble upon a samurai who will use the sword wisely. Includes a historical overview of sword making in ancient Japan.

Sadako (Japan) | Eleanor Coerr; illustrated by Ed Young

Only a toddler when the bomb fell on Hiroshima, Sadako is like most twelve-year-old girls: energetic and full of life. A star runner for her school, she finds herself becoming dizzy during races. A doctor diagnoses the girl with leukemia—"the atom-bomb disease." She begins folding one thousand paper cranes in the hope of becoming well again. After Sadako dies, her friends finish the cranes and bury them with her. *Note: Buddhist beliefs mentioned*

The Tale of the Mandarin Ducks (Japan)
Katherine Paterson; illustrated by Leo & Diane Dillon

In this Japanese folktale, a cruel village lord captures a beautiful drake. In captivity, the drake mourns for his mate and loses all his beauty. Feeling sorry for the bird, a kitchen maid sets him free. When her deed is discovered, both she and the lord's chief steward are sentenced to death. An unlikely pair of rescuers comes to their aid.

Tsunami! (Japan) | Kimiko Kajikawa; illustrated by Ed Young

As the oldest and wealthiest man in the village, Ojiisan has lived through many earthquakes and storms. But one day he senses something more dangerous on the way—a tsunami! As the sea begins to recede, he must quickly alert the community. He sets his valuable rice field alight to get their attention. The villagers run to put out the fire, safe from the monster wave.

The Korean Cinderella (Korea)
Shirley Climo; illustrated by Ruth Heller

Pear Blossom lives with her stepmother and stepsister. Jealous of her beauty, they force her to do impossible tasks. She succeeds at each one, however, thanks to the help of magical animals. Her character is also rewarded when she wins the hand of the magistrate.

Filipino Children's Favorite Stories (Philippines)
Liana Romulo; illustrated by Joanne de Leon

These thirteen classic Filipino folktales deliver moral lessons as they introduce readers to characters dealing with greed, laziness, love, and the consequences of life choices. Stories include "Why Mosquitoes Buzz Around Our Ears," "The Magic Lake," "The Deer and the Snail," and more.

ASIAN BOOKS FOR AGES 10-12

Chu Ju's House (China) | Gloria Whelan

Chu Ju's parents desperately want a son, so they're devastated when they have another baby daughter. In rural China, the government only allows families two children. To try again for a boy, they must get rid of the new infant. But fourteen-year-old Chu Ju won't let that happen to her sister, so she runs away to make a new life for herself instead.

The Diary of Ma Yan: The Struggles and Hopes of a Chinese Schoolgirl (China) | Ma Yan & Pierre Haski

More than anything else, thirteen-year-old Ma Yan wants an education. Her hopes crumble the day Mother pulls her aside to explain they can only afford school fees for her brothers. Ma Yan begins a journal, scribbling down her frustration, hunger, and poverty. Her family delivers the diary to a visiting journalist, who shares it with the world and helps change lives in Ma Yan's province. Inspiring!

Homesick: My Own Story (China) | Jean Fritz—Newbery Honor

A fictionalized autobiography, *Homesick* tells Jean Fritz's story of growing up as an American in 1920s China. Foreigners were looked on with suspicion at the time, and Jean recalls her childhood with the mixed emotions of living in one place while being desperately homesick for America—a land she doesn't really know but longs for.

The House of Sixty Fathers (China) | Meindert DeJong;
illustrated by Maurice Sendak—Newbery Honor

Tien Pao has escaped from the Japanese army, fleeing in a boat on the river. But a terrible rainstorm at night carries him straight back to occupied territory—with only his pet pig for company. Now Tien Pao must begin a long search for safety, home, and family.

Revolution Is Not a Dinner Party (China) | Ying Chang Compestine

Ling lives in China with her parents, both of whom work as doctors at the best hospital in Wuhan. She enjoys evenings spent laughing together and learning English, until an officer from the Communist Party moves into their apartment and later arrests her father. Will she ever see him again?

Starry River of the Sky (China) | Grace Lin

After running away, Rendi finds himself stranded in the Village of Clear Sky—a community with no moon. He takes a job as the innkeeper's chore boy, a position that introduces him to the villagers' problems and stories. Slowly Rendi starts to piece together exactly where the moon has gone and what it will take to return it. A fascinating companion to *Where the Mountain Meets the Moon* (below).

Tofu Quilt (China) | Ching Yeung Russell

This collection of poems in free verse tells the story of Yeung Ying, a girl from Hong Kong who visits her uncle and his family in mainland China. She hopes to become a writer, but must battle for her dreams in a society that doesn't place high value on educating girls. An inspiring read based on the author's own life.

GLOBAL PERSPECTIVE

How do you give your children the world in your home?

"When we lived in the States, we became friends with a neighboring family who was from another country. We spent different holidays together, tried foods, and just got to know each other. They made the things we read about in books come alive. It also gave our family the opportunity to learn to be respectful of other cultures and beliefs. Their family has since moved back to their home country, and we have moved overseas as well, but we still keep in touch. " Kimberly, Philippines

---

Where the Mountain Meets the Moon (China)
Grace Lin—Newbery Honor

Lin weaves traditional Chinese folklore into this fantasy account of Fruitless Mountain. Minli dwells on its peak in a tiny, mud-colored home with her parents.

Desperate to change the family's fortune, she embarks on a journey to find the Old Man on the Moon, said to hold the answer to all of life's questions.

Boys without Names (India) | Kashmira Sheth

Eleven-year-old Gopal lives in rural India, but after a year of bad crops and mounting debts, his father thinks their only hope lies in Mumbai. Eager to help the family after their move, Gopal follows a stranger to a factory job, only to find a sweatshop instead. Trapped alongside other boys making picture frames with toxic materials, Gopal forms deep friendships—and plots to help them all escape.

The Conch Bearer (India) | Chitra Banerjee Divakaruni

This fantasy adventure weaves descriptions of India's cities and countryside, folktales, and traditions into the life story of twelve-year-old Anand. After Anand shows an old man a kindness, the man invites the boy to journey with him across the country, battling enemies to return a magical conch shell to its rightful home in the mountains.

Homeless Bird (India) | Gloria Whelan

Thirteen-year-old Koly naturally feels nervous about meeting her new husband. But her situation goes from bad to worse when she finds out that the marriage is a scam—the in-laws only want a dowry so they can take their sick son on a pilgrimage. He dies and the family abandons Koly, but her fierce determination allows her to emerge stronger and more independent than ever. *Homeless Bird* tackles the issue of arranged marriages and the fate of teenage widows in India. *Note: Hindu beliefs mentioned*

Heart of a Samurai (Japan) | Margi Preus—Newbery Honor

Based on a true story, *Heart of a Samurai* follows fourteen-year-old Manjiro, whose fishing boat shipwrecks on a deserted island in 1841. The fishermen cannot return to Japan, as it remains closed to the outside world. Instead they travel to the United States, and Manjiro begins a new life. Years later he makes it back to his homeland, spends time in prison, and attempts to convince the emperor to open Japan's borders. See *Shipwrecked* by Rhoda Blumberg (page 120) for another version of Manjiro's story.

Mieko and the Fifth Treasure (Japan) | Eleanor Coerr

Mieko's art teacher says the "fifth treasure," beauty in the heart, makes the girl's calligraphy work so lovely. But her talent and her world shatter when the bomb drops on Nagasaki, badly injuring her hand. Even worse than her physical pain, the anger Mieko feels convinces her she has lost the fifth treasure forever. With the help of family and friends, she starts a healing journey to see if she can discover it again.

Hiroshima (Japan) | Laurence Yep

Twelve-year-old Sachi's life changes irrevocably the day the atomic bomb falls on Hiroshima. Badly burned, she survives, but her sister and father die. She spends years in hiding, as those who move to the city don't want to be reminded of the war. Then Sachi travels to America for plastic surgery, returning with the hope of helping other victims. *Note: Goes into detail about the release of the atomic bomb and its effects*

Sadako and the Thousand Paper Cranes (Japan)
Eleanor Coerr; illustrated by Ronald Himler

Sadako looks like a healthy eleven-year-old, but it turns out she has leukemia as a result of radiation exposure from the bomb dropped on Hiroshima when she was a baby. Taking a classmate's advice, Sadako begins folding one thousand paper cranes in the hope that her prayers for healing will be answered. *Note: Buddhist beliefs mentioned*

Shipwrecked! The True Adventures of a Japanese Boy (Japan)
Rhoda Blumberg

Blumberg recounts the tale of a boy whose fishing boat shipwrecks off the coast of Japan. The country's law at the time states that no one who leaves may return without being put to death, so Manjiro sails to the United States with the whaling boat that rescues him. After receiving an education, he eventually goes back to Japan and becomes an honored samurai. See *Heart of a Samurai* by Margi Preus (page 119) for another version of Manjiro's story.

The Kite Fighters (Korea) | Linda Sue Park

Brothers Kee-sup and Young-sup love kites. Kee-sup enjoys creating them and his younger brother can maneuver them with artistry and skill. The king chooses

Young-sup to participate in the New Year kite-flying competition, but the brothers' father—and the cultural tradition of the time—insist the honor of competing must go to the eldest brother instead.

Seesaw Girl (Korea) | Linda Sue Park

As a daughter in a wealthy family, Jade knows she must stay within the walls of the Inner Court until she marries. Yet the stories she's heard about life on the other side—about freedom and adventure—lead her to imagine, and long for, what she might be missing.

A Single Shard (Korea) | Linda Sue Park—Newbery Medal

Set in twelfth-century Korea, *A Single Shard* chronicles the life of Tree Ear, an orphan living under a bridge with a homeless man. Fascinated by the local potter, Tree Ear eventually becomes an apprentice. He travels to the royal court in the hopes of gaining a commission for his master. But after a long and dangerous expedition, will he still have what it takes to impress the imperial pottery expert?

Year of Impossible Goodbyes (Korea) | Sook Nyul Choi

It's 1945 and Sookan lives in North Korea, currently occupied by the Japanese. Her father and brothers away in labor camps, she works in a factory making socks for the army with other female relatives. The thought of eventual freedom keeps them going in the midst of fear and the loss of their identity. Yet the end of the war only brings a different type of domination by Russian communists. Sookan, her brother, and her mother determine to escape to the south.

GLOBAL PERSPECTIVE

How do you give your children the world in your home?

"Our kids have enjoyed Story of the World, which has introduced them to many countries through a historical perspective. We also check out DVDs about children living in different places. At Christmas we learned about Christmas customs in other countries." Marnita, Canada

Goodbye, Vietnam (Vietnam) | Gloria Whelan

Times are hard for thirteen-year-old Mai, who drops out of school to work in the rice paddies. And they go from bad to worse when government soldiers appear and threaten to arrest her grandmother for practicing traditional medicine. The family feels they have no choice but to flee in the night, so her father secures their passage to Hong Kong. They board with little money or food but with hopes of finding prosperity in the city.

Inside Out and Back Again (Vietnam)
Thanhha Lai—Newbery Honor

Ha has spent all ten years of her life in Saigon and knows it well. She understands the food, the marketplace, and her friends. Then wartime reaches its way into the corners of her steady life and uproots everything. Forced to flee, Ha finds herself on a ship going somewhere she can't understand—Alabama. In free verse Lai describes the bullying, racism, and other challenges Ha must overcome to create a new identity.

The Land I Lost: Adventures of a Boy in Vietnam (Vietnam)
Quang Nhuong Huynh; illustrated by Vo-Dinh Mai

Explore Vietnam's countryside through fifteen chapters—each one a unique snapshot of the author's rural childhood. Wild and domestic animals (including his pet water buffalo, Tank), relatives, and friends play a featured role alongside plenty of adventure and danger. Also check out *Water Buffalo Days: Growing Up in Vietnam* by the same author.

When Heaven Fell (Vietnam) | Carolyn Marsden

Binh wishes she could go to school, but instead she must sit by the loud, crowded road selling sodas and fruit. Her life contains few surprises, so it shocks the whole family when her grandmother announces that decades ago she had a child with an American soldier—a daughter sent to the States at the age of five. Binh's aunt, now grown, wants to come for a visit.

CHAPTER 9

SILENT MUSIC: MIDDLE EAST

Countries/regions included in this chapter: Afghanistan, Egypt, Iraq, Israel, Lebanon, Pakistan, Palestine

Note: Since many of the books in this chapter deal with the conflicts in this region of the world, I've chosen to begin this book list with ages 6–8 instead of ages 4–6. I suggest previewing titles first to determine when they're appropriate for your kids.

Trishna recently decided to write a report about another country as a home-school project. We sat at the dining table side by side, cups of tea in our hands, as she tossed out possible locations. Her birthplace of India was, of course, a high contender, but after a few moments she said, "I'd like to study Iran." Her interest had nothing to do with attempting to understand Middle Eastern conflicts. Her desire to learn was just that—a curiosity about a fascinating place. We looked up facts online and checked out library books to aid her research. When she had completed her report, she read it to the family one night after dinner. The experience reminded me once again that children don't think in terms of "us and them." They see other people as potential friends no matter where they come from. You'll find that the books on this list help you view this area of the world—and those who live there—through that compassionate lens as well.

MIDDLE EASTERN BOOKS FOR AGES 6–8

Nasreen's Secret School: A True Story from Afghanistan (Afghanistan) | Jeanette Winter

Nasreen hasn't spoken since her parents disappeared. Her grandmother remembers life before the Taliban banned girls from receiving an education or venturing out without a chaperone. Determined to help, Grandmother takes Nasreen to a "secret school." The young girl's studies free her mind from her sadness, and free her lips to speak again.

Day of Ahmed's Secret (Egypt) | Florence Parry Heide & Judith Heide Gilliland; illustrated by Ted Lewin

Ahmed can't wait to share a secret with his family, but first he must finish the day's work delivering propane to customers throughout Cairo's busy streets. Eventually he arrives home, bursting with a proud announcement: he has learned to write his name! Delightful illustrations.

The Egyptian Cinderella (Egypt) Shirley Climo; illustrated by Ruth Heller

This title finds its original source in the true story of a Greek slave girl, Rhodopis, who married a Pharaoh around 500 BC. Because of her heritage and position as a servant, the other Egyptian girls initially scorn and tease Rhodopis. One day a falcon carries her golden slipper to the Pharaoh himself, and the search for the girl who fits the tiny shoe begins. *Note: Featured in the story is Horus, the traditional Egyptian god of the sky*

The Librarian of Basra: A True Story from Iraq (Iraq) | Jeanette Winter

As war comes closer, Alia the librarian will do anything to protect the thirty thousand books in her care. Moving them under the cover of night, she saves them all just a few days before the entire library burns to the ground. As she works, Alia imagines an end to the fighting for her people. *Note: Storyline centers around war, with bombs and guns depicted in the illustrations*

Silent Music: A Story of Baghdad (Iraq) | James Rumford

Like many young boys his age, Ali loves soccer and music. But he also has a unique interest—the ancient art of calligraphy. Growing up during a troubled time in Iraq, Ali uses his talent to escape fears of the war around him. *Note: Portrays war from a child's perspective with mentions of bombs, missiles, and death*

GLOBAL PERSPECTIVE

How do you give your children the world in your home?

"I grew up in a very diverse area, but my children are not. So I like to introduce nonfiction and fiction books with protagonists from a variety of cultures, ethnicities, and economic statuses to broaden their perspective. We also read a lot of history books and maps. At a young age, my children are fascinated by other cultures—near and far." Beth, Pennsylvania

---

Sami and the Time of Troubles (Lebanon) | Florence Parry Heide & Judith Heide Gilliland; illustrated by Ted Lewin

Sami loves listening to stories of what life was like before war reached Beirut. While he spends most of his time in hiding with family, he imagines his father's peach orchard—wondering if the fruit still grows there. His grandfather inspires the boy to join with others his age in a march for peace. Lovely illustrations.

How Many Donkeys? An Arabic Counting Tale (Middle East) Margaret MacDonald & Nadia Taibah; illustrated by Carol Liddiment

Jouha loads his ten donkeys with the dates he hopes to sell at the market. But as he climbs onto one of the animals, it suddenly seems as though a donkey has disappeared. Youngsters will giggle as they watch Jouha forget one donkey again and again—and they'll learn to count to ten in Arabic at the same time!

Listen to the Wind: The Story of Dr. Greg and Three Cups of Tea (Pakistan) | Greg Mortenson

Colorful collages form the backdrop for this picture book describing Greg Mortenson's work building schools in Pakistan. After villagers help him recover from illness, he wants to return their kindness. The wise man he asks for suggestions tells him to "listen to the wind" to find out what to do.

Sitti and the Cats: A Tale of Friendship (Palestine)
Sally Bahous Allen; illustrated by Nancy Malick

In this traditional Palestinian folktale, we meet Sitti—an old woman living in a small village. Though poor, she doesn't hesitate to help others when she can. But one winter, Sitti finds herself cold and alone. While collecting fuel for a fire, she frees a cat stuck in a tree. This selfless act leads Sitti to her just reward, enough for herself with plenty leftover to share.

Sitti's Secrets (Palestine)
Naomi Shihab Nye; illustrated by Nancy Carpenter

Sitti travels with her father across the world to visit her grandmother, who lives in Palestine. Young Sitti falls in love with her extended family members and their culture, and they communicate well even without speaking the same language. When Sitti returns to the United States, she writes a letter to the president—expressing her hope for peace in the world.

MIDDLE EASTERN BOOKS FOR AGES 8–10

Four Feet, Two Sandals (Afghanistan/Pakistan) | Karen Lynn Williams & Khadra Mohammed; illustrated by Doug Chayka

Refugees of war with their families, Lina and Feroza meet one day when a relief worker drops used clothes off the back of a truck. Digging quickly through the pile, each girl comes away with one new sandal from a matching pair. Their decision to take turns sharing the sandals leads to friendship.

Ancient Egypt: An Interactive History Adventure (Egypt)
Heather Adamson

Explore ancient Egypt by choosing your own path within this story. You must make several decisions that lead to riches or to certain death. Also includes an overview of the time period and a helpful glossary. If your kids enjoy this title, check out the others in the series. *Note: Religious beliefs mentioned*

Mummies Made in Egypt (Egypt) | Aliki

A well-told and illustrated introduction to the process of mummification for young learners. The book explains why Egyptians wrapped their dead, how they did it, and the final outcome after a mummy was completed. *Note: Religious beliefs mentioned*

Pharaoh's Boat (Egypt) | David L. Weitzman

Thousands of years ago, Pharaoh Cheops commissioned a pyramid that would house his remains. When he died, his son ordered a magnificent boat built to transport his father. This is the story of what happened in 1954 when the boat was discovered and rebuilt by historians—fascinating! *Note: Religious beliefs mentioned*

Voices of Ancient Egypt (Egypt)
Kay Winters; illustrated by Barry Moser

This book by National Geographic offers portraits of ancient Egyptian workers, combined with illustrations and poems that explain their occupations. The snapshots give a personal look on an ancient civilization—describing the jobs of the farmer, pyramid builder, weaver, and even the embalmer. *Note: Religious beliefs mentioned*

Alia's Mission: Saving the Books of Iraq (Iraq) | Mark Alan Stamaty

Told in graphic novel form, *Alia's Mission* recounts the story of the chief librarian in Basra, Iraq, for older readers. As war draws closer, Alia pleads with government officials to move the city's collection of books out of harm's way. When they refuse, she comes up with a plan to take matters into her own hands and smuggle the books to safety. Inspiring!

Snow in Jerusalem (Israel) | Deborah da Costa;
illustrated by Cornelius Van Wright & Ying-Hwa Hu

Avi and Hamudi both call Jerusalem home—Avi lives in the Jewish Quarter and Hamudi in the Muslim Quarter. Their lives converge when both begin to care for a stray cat that leads them to each other, to her newborn kittens, and to peace, as rare snow begins to blanket the city. *Note: Religious beliefs mentioned*

One Green Apple (Middle East/U.S.)
Eve Bunting; illustrated by Ted Lewin

It's Farah's second day at her new school, and this morning the class is going to an apple orchard. Feeling self-conscious because of her language and head covering, Farah plucks one lonely green apple among all the red ones. As she watches the apples blend together in a cider, Farah gathers courage that she will also blend and belong someday.

MIDDLE EASTERN BOOKS FOR AGES 10–12

Afghan Dreams: Young Voices of Afghanistan (Afghanistan)
Michael Sullivan; photographs by Tony O'Brien

This title pairs photographs with stories of children in Afghanistan, providing readers a personal connection to this war-torn country. The pages follow kids from a variety of different backgrounds and ethnicities, giving a snapshot of their daily lives and hopes for their country and future. *Note: Religious beliefs mentioned*

The Breadwinner (Afghanistan) | Deborah Ellis

Parvana lives in an abandoned apartment building in Kabul. When the Taliban arrest her well-educated father, she develops a plan to care for her remaining family members. Since women are not allowed to go to school or work outside the home, she disguises herself in her dead brother's clothes in order to earn money.

Extra Credit (Afghanistan)
Andrew Clements; illustrated by Mark Elliott

Abby is an American girl who loves nature and climbing mountains. School and homework? Not so much. But when she finds out she may need to repeat sixth grade, she takes on an extra-credit project—writing to a pen pal in another country. When Abby's first letter arrives in Afghanistan, the village elders can't decide who should respond. What begins with reluctance on both sides leads to a deeper understanding of two cultures.

GLOBAL PERSPECTIVE

How do you give your children the world in your home?

"I was born in Scotland and raised in Toronto. My parents were born in India, but grew up in Pakistan and now live in Toronto. My husband, in Ohio, joined the military when he was nineteen. Every deployment as my son got older was a discussion starting with our globe to see where Papa was. Our home is filled with languages including Urdu, Arabic, and English, with bits of Spanish and French and strong swooshes of American and Canadian friendly rivalries." Omaira, Arizona

Shooting Kabul (Afghanistan) | N. H. Senzai

Fadi's parents have decided to emigrate to the United States. In the rush to escape from Taliban soldiers, however, the boy's younger sister gets left behind. The grief-stricken family arrives in the United States just a few months before September 11, complicating their transition to a new culture. Determined to find his sister, Fadi enters a photography competition in the hopes of winning the grand-prize trip abroad. *Note: Religious beliefs mentioned*

Cleopatra VII: Daughter of the Nile, Egypt, 57 BC (Egypt)
Kristiana Gregory

Open this book to read Cleopatra's fictional diary entries from ages twelve to fourteen—a tumultuous time in the princess's life. Her father is in hiding due to death threats, and Cleopatra must deal with adolescence and jealous sisters as she prepares to one day assume the throne. Also includes a timeline of the queen's latter years as well as a family tree. If this is a hit with your tweens, look for the other titles in the Royal Diaries Series. *Note: Religious beliefs mentioned*

Iqbal (Pakistan) | Francesco D'Adamo

Iqbal arrives at a carpet factory and meets other child slaves working to pay off their families' debts. The boy shocks them by revealing that their master has no intention of releasing them—ever. Iqbal continues to hope for freedom and courageously works to secure a way of escape. Based on the remarkable true story of Iqbal Masih, who gave his life fearlessly to help others. *Note: Religious beliefs mentioned*

Three Cups of Tea: One Man's Journey to Change the World . . . One Child at a Time (Young Reader's Edition) (Pakistan)
Greg Mortenson & David Oliver Relin; adapted by Sarah Thomson

The popular memoir revised for middle-grade readers, *Three Cups of Tea* traces Greg Mortenson's journey to build schools for a small village in Pakistan. Includes an interesting interview with the author's twelve-year-old daughter as well as photos arranged in a scrapbook style.

CHAPTER 10

WAGON WHEELS: NORTH AMERICA

Countries/cultures included in this chapter: African American, Canada, Native American, United States

In the summer of 2014, our family embarked on our first extended road trip in the United States. Inspired by the Little House on the Prairie book series by Laura Ingalls Wilder, we headed west to explore sites in Wisconsin, Minnesota, and South Dakota where the real Ingalls family once lived. Jonathan and I even waded in Plum Creek together, like Laura and Mary before us (minus the leeches!), and we drove several extra hours to visit Mt. Rushmore as well.

Two adults, three children, eight days, seven hotels, and over two thousand miles in a van—at times we thought the experience amazing and at times we thought we must be crazy. Now that both the magic and the madness of the trip are over, I know we'll never forget the summer when U.S. history and literature came alive for us. Maybe a book in this chapter's list will lead to an unforgettable road trip of your own.

NORTH AMERICAN BOOKS FOR AGES 4-6

My People (African American)
Langston Hughes; photographs by Charles R. Smith, Jr.

My People uses stunning black-and-white photos as the backdrop for a famous Langston Hughes poem by the same name. It honors diversity among African Americans by including different shades of skin color and different ages—from the sweetness of a newborn baby to the steadiness of a grandpa's wrinkled hands.

Shades of Black: A Celebration of Our Children (African American)
Sandra L. Pinkney; photographs by Myles C. Pinkney

Beginning with the phrase "I am black; I am unique," this book launches into a photographic celebration of African American children—their shades, hair, eyes, and pride. Trishna, Elijah, and I flipped through the pages to match their own skin colors, which were compared to the "midnight blue of a licorice stick" and the "velvety orange in a peach."

ABC of Canada (Canada)
Kim Bellefontaine; illustrated by Per Henrik Gurth

This alphabetical book introduces little ones to the famous landmarks and pastimes of Canada—including the Northern Lights, the Yukon, winter sports, and more.

A Mountain Alphabet (Canada)
Margriet Ruurs; illustrated by Andrew Kiss

Use this book to introduce your littles to the natural beauty found in the mountains of western North America. It features twenty-six stunning paintings (one for each letter), paired with a line of alliterative text to read aloud. You can also play "I spy" on every page, searching for plants and animals that begin with the highlighted letter.

Ten Little Rabbits (Native American)
Virginia Grossman; illustrated by Sylvia Long

Learn to count to ten alongside the rabbits in this story—each one engaged in Native American cultural traditions including weaving, fishing, and storytelling. Every number represents a different tribe, explained in further detail in the afterword.

Thanks to the Animals (Native American)
Allen Sockabasin; illustrated by Rebekah Raye

Based on the winter migration of the Passmaquoddy tribe, this title introduces us to baby Zoo-Sap, who falls off his family's sled during their move to a new location. All the forest animals gather around the infant to protect and warm him until his father returns. Littles will adore the pictures of these gentle creatures in the woods!

If You're Not from the Prairie (U.S.)
David Bouchard; illustrated by Henry Ripplinger

A born-and-bred prairie boy explains what makes his part of the country so special. He introduces us to the sun, wind, and sky he knows and loves in these short verses paired with gorgeous illustrations that make me want to move to the prairie, too!

This Land Is Your Land (U.S.)
Woody Guthrie; illustrated by Kathy Jakobsen

Guthrie's popular folksong lyrics, now an American anthem, stand paired here with oil paintings showcasing the beauty of the widespread landscape—as well as issues like homelessness and poverty within our land. Moving for children *and* parents.

GLOBAL PERSPECTIVE

How do you give your children the world in your home?

"We live in one of the most diverse zip codes in the U.S. The culture, ethnicity, languages, and economics are all very different from middle class America, and I am so very grateful my children are in the midst of it all." Kate, Washington State

One Morning in Maine (U.S.)
Robert McCloskey—Caldecott Honor

Follow Sal and her baby sister as she excitedly wakes and gets ready for a voyage to Buck's Harbor with her father, only to realize she has a loose tooth. Concerned it might derail her plans, Sal ends up learning a valuable lesson about flexibility that makes the trip even better.

The Scrambled States of America (U.S.) | Laurie Keller

Kansas is bored, always stuck in the middle of the country. He decides to host a party so the states can mingle, at which Idaho and Virginia decide to swap places for a while. Other states follow, leading to chaos until they figure out how to unscramble themselves. Laugh-out-loud funny. (Also look for the board game, inspired by the book, for ages six and up!)

NORTH AMERICAN BOOKS FOR AGES 6–8

Freedom Summer (African American)
Deborah Wiles; illustrated by Jerome Lagarrigue

A book to use when you're ready to broach the subject of segregation, *Freedom Summer* describes the friendship between light-skinned Joe and dark-skinned John Henry. The boys spend every moment together—except at the town pool, which is for whites only. When a new law opens the pool to everyone, they excitedly rush over, only to find that it takes more than a law to bring true change.

Martin's Big Words: The Life of Dr. Martin Luther King, Jr. (African American) | Doreen Rappaport; illustrated by Bryan Collier—Caldecott Honor

This title's sparse text highlights the "big" words from Martin Luther King's speeches, mixed with prose describing his life and death. Stunning illustrations feature stained glass window patterns that tell a story all their own. It doesn't shy away from the harshness of segregation—preview to make sure your kids are ready before reading together. *Note: Christian beliefs mentioned*

The Other Side (African American)
Jacqueline Woodson; illustrated by E. B. Lewis

Clover and Annie live on opposite sides of the same fence, and their parents say it isn't "safe" to cross over. Why not? Clover's family is black and Annie's is white. Their parents didn't make any rules, however, against sitting *on* the fence itself, which is where the girls spend the summer in this hopeful story of friendship.

The Story of Ruby Bridges (African American)
Robert Coles; illustrated by George Ford

As the first black child chosen to attend a white elementary school, first-grader Ruby Bridges must walk past an angry mob every day to get to class. Months pass and Ruby's teacher wonders where the girl gets her strength—until the day she sees Ruby stop and speak directly to those who hate her. So moving. *Note: Christian beliefs mentioned*

Uncle Jed's Barbershop (African American)
Margaree King Mitchell; illustrated by James E. Ransome

Themes of segregation, perseverance, and generosity gently weave together in the touching story of Uncle Jed, whose dream of opening his own barbershop finally comes true at the age of seventy-nine. Though decades pass before he achieves his goal, his commitment to his vision—and his family—never wavers.

Unspoken: A Story from the Underground Railroad (African American)
Henry Cole

In this wordless picture book, readers watch a young girl discover a runaway slave hiding on her farm in Virginia. As armed Confederate troops make their way through the area to find him, she has a difficult choice to make. A lengthy afterword adds context to this courageous account.

Wagon Wheels (African American)
Barbara Brenner; illustrated by Don Bolognese

The Muldie family, African American pioneers, journey west seeking free land, only to face the pain of their mother's death on the trip. Father decides to look for a better homestead, asking his three sons to stay by themselves until he sends word. When a letter and map finally arrive, the boys must make their way—on their own—to join him. Inspired by a remarkable true story.

M Is for Maple: A Canadian Alphabet (Canada)
Mike Ulmer; illustrated by Melanie Rose

This alphabetical introduction to Canada for slightly older children offers readers a tour of the country—making sure they know about Anne with an *e*, popular sports, as well as other historical and cultural details. Interesting—I learned plenty!

Jingle Dancer (Native American) | Cynthia Leitich Smith; illustrated by Cornelius Van Wright & Ying-Hwa Hu

Watching the home movie of Grandma's jingle dance performed long ago, Jenna wishes she could join in at the next powwow. But there isn't enough time to order the tin jingles that make the dress sing. One by one, female family members donate their bells to make the girl's dream come true. An author's note explains this native tradition.

The Legend of the Indian Paintbrush (Native American)
Tomie dePaola

Little Gopher has always been smaller than the rest of the boys in his tribe—so he can't run, wrestle, or become a warrior. Then one day he has a vision in which he discovers his own mission—to paint the sunset. *Note: Native American religious beliefs mentioned*

When Clay Sings (Native American)
Byrd Baylor; illustrated by Tom Bahti—Caldecott Honor

When Native American children find broken pieces of pottery in their desert village, they imagine the lives of their ancestors. Parents remind the children to treat the treasures with respect—because each piece of pottery has its own voice, song, and story. *Note: Native American religious beliefs mentioned*

Brothers at Bat: The True Story of an Amazing All-Brother Baseball Team (U.S.) | Audry Vernick; illustrated by Steven Salerno

This incredible true story introduces readers to the Acerra family and their sixteen children, including twelve boys who make up an entire baseball team in New Jersey. Follow them from boyhood to adults who serve in World War II, continuing to play ball after their return home. The Acerra brothers were even honored by the Baseball Hall of Fame.

GLOBAL PERSPECTIVE

How do you give your children the world in your home?

"We incorporate multiple cultures in nearly everything in our goal to raise a world citizen: through travel, music, food, literature, language, and movies. My daughter has visited Italy, Ireland, Canada, and Mexico and speaks dashes of Spanish, French, Italian, and Russian. Cultural festivals like Chinese New Year go on the agenda whenever possible."
Barbara, Alabama

Chang's Paper Pony (U.S.)
Eleanor Coerr; illustrated by Deborah Kogan Ray

Chang lives in San Francisco during the Gold Rush and works with his Chinese grandpa in a hotel kitchen. The young boy feels ostracized in the new world and longs for a pony as a friend. But the only horse Grandpa can afford is a paper one that hangs on the wall. *Chang's Paper Pony* celebrates the joy of a longed-for wish that finally comes true. Also look for *Buffalo Bill and the Pony Express* by the same author. Both books make good early readers.

Dumpling Soup (U.S.)
Jama Kim Rattigan; illustrated by Lillian Hsu-Flanders

Marisa's family, made up of a blend of different cultures, lives in Hawaii. Each New Year's Eve, the women get together to prepare homemade dumplings as part of their annual celebration. Seven-year-old Marisa excitedly receives her first invitation to help make the traditional meal, but she worries her dumplings won't be good enough.

Dust for Dinner (U.S.) | Ann Turner; illustrated by Robert Barrett

Jake and Maggy love their family's farm in Oklahoma. But when the rains stop and the dust comes, hard times lie ahead. Their parents make the tough decision to auction the land and head west to California, where they hope a new life will enable them to start again. This lovely early reader tackles the Great Depression, yet still manages to maintain an optimistic tone.

Little House on the Prairie Series (U.S.)
Laura Ingalls Wilder; illustrated by Garth Williams

What U.S. book list could possibly be complete without the inclusion of Laura Ingalls Wilder's series about prairie life in the late 1800s? I've read through these books twice with my children—once when they were in the six- to eight-year age range, and once in the eight- to ten-year range. Without a doubt we got more out of it the second time, yet the books have a timeless quality that makes them appeal to younger listeners as well. *Note: These titles highlight the realities of pioneer life: strong tensions with Native Americans, conversations about massacres, people freezing in blizzards, and so on. As you read aloud, you can certainly edit any passages that don't seem like a match for your child's age.*

The Long Way to a New Land (U.S.) | Joan Sandin

Carl Erik's father has given up on the family's farm in Sweden. If they stay much longer, they'll starve. Then a letter arrives from an uncle in the new land that promises possibilities, freedom, and opportunity. Can hope be just a long steamship ride away? Follow the family's story further in the sequel, *The Long Way Westward*. Both titles are part of the I Can Read Series for early readers.

Moonshot: The Flight of Apollo 11 (U.S.) | Brian Floca

I learned so much from this well-penned tribute to the Apollo space program and its first victory. Describing the voyage in short verses, Brian Floca allows those of us not alive at the time to feel as though we were—breathing a sigh of relief alongside the families watching on their black-and-white televisions when the astronauts land safely.

A Picture Book of . . . Series (U.S.) | David A. Adler

My daughter once picked *A Picture Book of Harriet Tubman* as her favorite read-aloud, so clearly this collection is a huge hit in our home! They allow your little one to meet well-known individuals from U.S. history for the first time—including Benjamin Franklin, George Washington Carver, Jackie Robinson, Thomas Edison, and many more. I especially enjoy the focus on the childhoods of these famous world-changers.

Prairie School (U.S.) | Avi; illustrated by Bill Farnsworth

Why does Noah even need to learn how to read? That's exactly what the frustrated nine-year-old wonders when his aunt arrives to teach him on the family's new farm. He's perfectly happy with his daily work under the open prairie sky, but Noah slowly realizes that the pages in books have even more freedom to offer him.

Sam the Minuteman (U.S.)
Nathaniel Benchley; illustrated by Arnold Lobel

The British are coming, and Sam's father wakes him with the urgent command to gather the guns and get ready. Introduce your kids to the American Revolution through Sam's eyes as he experiences the historic battles at Lexington and Concord. For a British boy's perspective on the event, look for *George the Drummer Boy* by the same author. *Note: Illustrations depict the wounded and dead*

The Thanksgiving Story (U.S.)
Alice Dalgliesh; illustrated by Helen Sewell—Caldecott Honor

Experience the Thanksgiving story through the eyes of Giles, Constance, and Damaris Hopkins—children on board the Mayflower. They describe meeting their baby brother, Oceanus (born on the ship), building the new settlement, and the harvest celebration after the hard winter. *Note: Christian beliefs mentioned*

This Is New York (U.S.) | Miroslav Sasek

First published in the 1960s, this title in Sasek's classic series highlights the bustle of Times Square, different ethnicities, and tall skyscrapers. Fun facts are included that older readers will enjoy as well—like the number of elevators in the city and the number of fires each day. Make sure you also check out *This Is San Francisco*, *This Is Texas*, and *This Is Washington, D.C.*

NORTH AMERICAN BOOKS FOR AGES 8-10

Allen Jay and the Underground Railroad (African American)
Marlene Targ Brill; illustrated by Janice Lee Porter

After Isaac Jay receives word that a runaway slave is coming to their Quaker village for help, he asks his son Allen to hide the man in their cornfields. Eleven-year-old Allen does so, risking his life in a dangerous overnight journey to freedom.

Aunt Harriet's Underground Railroad in the Sky (African American)
Faith Ringgold

In a story that combines fact with fantasy, Cassie learns about slavery and finds her way to freedom by retracing the route of the Underground Railroad—with "Aunt Harriet" Tubman as her guide. Cassie hopes to reunite with Aunt Harriet and her brother BeBe *if* she can make it to their destination safely.

Follow the Drinking Gourd (African American) | Jeanette Winter

Peg Leg Jo works for the plantation owner by day, but his hidden passion is helping slaves escape. He teaches a family of five the song "Follow the Drinking Gourd," which contains hidden clues to help them find the Underground Railroad and their route to safety in Canada.

GLOBAL PERSPECTIVE

How do you give your children the world in your home?

"The diversity of the city of Chicago makes it easy to introduce my boys to the world. The city has museums and neighborhoods dedicated to different cultures. Chicago has the largest Polish population outside of Poland. We also have the Chicago History Museum, a Lithuanian Museum, a Mexican-American Museum and many more. I give my boys 'history' lessons each time we pass through a particular neighborhood." Kendra, Illinois

---

The Gold Cadillac (African American) | Mildred D. Taylor

Nobody could be more surprised than Lois and Wilma (except perhaps their mother!) the day Father pulls into the driveway in a gold Cadillac. The neighbors admire it and the girls beam with pride. But when the African American family drives from Ohio to Mississippi, they find that a shiny new car in the South attracts suspicion and anger.

Henry's Freedom Box: A True Story from the Underground Railroad (African American)
Ellen Levine; illustrated by Kadir Nelson—Caldecott Honor

Slave Henry Brown is ready to take drastic measures for a chance at freedom. Now that his wife and children have been sold and taken away, he has nothing to lose. With the help of other abolitionists, Henry ships himself to the North in a wooden crate. Incredible true story.

Meet Addy: An American Girl (African American)
Connie Porter; illustrated by Dahl Taylor

Addy wakes one night and overhears her momma and poppa discussing plans to run away from the plantation where they are enslaved. Before they can leave, the master sells Addy's father and brother. Now Addy and Momma have to make the long, dangerous journey to Philadelphia alone. *Note: If your children enjoy Addy's story, check out other titles in the American Girls Series.*

Molly Bannaky (African American)
Alice McGill; illustrated by Chris K. Soentpiet

Dairymaid Molly Walsh receives a sentence of seven years as an indentured servant in America for accidentally spilling the milk. After earning her freedom in the New World, she falls in love with and marries a slave. Don't miss this remarkable true story of a lady who continued to prosper despite overwhelming challenges, going on to become the grandmother of scientist and abolitionist Benjamin Banneker!

Moses: When Harriet Tubman Led Her People to Freedom
(African American) | Carole Boston Weatherford;
illustrated by Kadir Nelson—Caldecott Honor

Harriet Tubman's faith takes center stage in this account of her life. Her prayers to the heavens, and God's responses, anchor the text and illustrations as she seeks guidance along each step of her sojourn. *Note: Christian beliefs mentioned*

Nettie's Trip South (African American)
Ann Turner; illustrated by Ronald Himler

Ten-year-old Nettie travels south for the first time and describes her trip in a letter to a friend. As she writes, Nettie shares about the train ride and other memorable details, but mostly she conveys her horror and disgust at the glimpses of slavery she experiences. A sobering, thought-provoking title for slightly older readers.

Sweet Clara and the Freedom Quilt (African American)
Deborah Hopkinson; illustrated by James Ransome

Clara dreams of a reunion with her momma, who works on another plantation, and of one day living together as a family. When she overhears two slaves discussing the Underground Railroad, Clara begins to piece together a map on a "freedom quilt" to help other slaves find their way after she escapes. Inspiring!

A Pioneer Sampler: The Daily Life of a Pioneer Family in 1840
(Canada) | Barbara Greenwood

Called a "must-have" by *Publisher's Weekly* for those interested in pioneer living, this story blends the life of the fictional Robertson family with facts about the time period. Get an inside glimpse of their daily routine (making butter, slaughtering hogs, baking bread) as well as the universal challenges of childhood (sibling rivalry, school, dealing with bullies). Look for the sequels, *A Pioneer Thanksgiving* and *A Pioneer Christmas*.

Salmon Creek (Canada)
Annette LeBox; illustrated by Karen Reczuch

Follow the life of the Pacific salmon in this picture book that introduces readers to one coho salmon named Sumi. Combining story, poetry, and science, *Salmon Creek* lets readers tag along from Sumi's birth to her adventurous travels in the sea and to her return as she prepares to die and the cycle continues. An afterword describes in detail the plight of wild salmon and how we can help their habitats live on as nature intended.

Brother Eagle, Sister Sky (Native American) | Susan Jeffers

Based on a speech delivered by Chief Seattle of the Suquamish upon signing a treaty, *Brother Eagle, Sister Sky* demonstrates the deep respect for nature within the Native American culture. The chief also includes a warning about the consequences for future generations if the earth is not cared for. *Note: Native American religious beliefs mentioned*

The Girl Who Loved Wild Horses (Native American)
Paul Goble—Caldecott Medal

Her tribe follows the buffalo, but this young Native American heroine has always felt closer to the wild horses. One day in the midst of a thunderstorm she is swept up in a horse stampede and begins to live among the animals she loves. Eventually the girl transforms into a beautiful mare. *Note: Native American religious beliefs mentioned*

Hawk, I'm Your Brother (Native American)
Byrd Baylor; illustrated by Peter Parnall—Caldecott Honor

Young Rudy desperately wants to fly, so he captures a baby hawk in the hopes of learning from it. But the boy slowly discovers that the best way to learn is to let go of his own goal—allowing his new pet to achieve its dreams. *Note: Native American religious beliefs mentioned*

Knots on a Counting Rope (Native American)
Bill Martin Jr. & John Archambault; illustrated by Ted Rand

Come sit around the campfire with a Native American grandfather and grandson. Sensing their time together may be nearing its final end, the boy asks his grandfather to tell the story of his birth. Knots on the counting rope represent the passing of time and finding the courage to accept one's own limitations, like the boy's blindness. *Note: Native American religious beliefs mentioned*

Powwow (Native American) | George Ancona

This photo essay gives readers a front-row seat at a modern powwow and an understanding of past and present Native American culture. Gorgeous full-color snapshots positively portray the dances, traditions, and importance of family at the annual Crow Fair in Montana. *Note: Native American religious beliefs mentioned*

Squanto's Journey: The Story of the First Thanksgiving (Native American) | Joseph Bruchac; illustrated by Greg Shed

Come see the story of Thanksgiving anew through the eyes of Squanto, without whom there may have never been a successful colony at Plymouth. His journey overseas to slavery in Spain and back again as a translator to the colonists features here. Add this to your Thanksgiving collection of titles for a more complete perspective on the holiday. *Note: Native American religious beliefs mentioned*

The Story of Jumping Mouse (Native American)
John Steptoe—Caldecott Honor

In this retelling of a Native American legend, a young mouse ventures on a dangerous journey to the distant and beautiful "far-off land." Along the way he meets other creatures in need of help, which he offers sacrificially. Finally Jumping Mouse receives great rewards for his unselfishness and a new name forever. *Note: Native American religious beliefs mentioned*

GLOBAL PERSPECTIVE

How do you give your children the world in your home?

"We make a habit of looking on clothes, toys, food products, and just about everything we buy to find out where they were made. We find a lot of 'Made in China,' of course, but also many other countries in Asia, Africa, South America, as well as the U.S. As the kids have gotten older, this has led to interesting conversations about buying local vs. buying from large corporations. We have also watched some interesting videos on YouTube about how crops grow in various places around the world. Since we do not live near many farms, it's been interesting to learn about where our food comes from—and also learn ways that people around the world are interdependent." Sue, New Jersey

Thirteen Moons on Turtle's Back (Native American)
Joseph Bruchac; illustrated by Thomas Locker

A Native American father explains to his son that the thirteen scales on a turtle's back correspond with the thirteen moons of the year. He goes on to tell the story of each moon, marking the seasons and the passing of time. I've always been a fan of Thomas Locker's paintings—they capture the natural world beautifully here.
Note: Native American religious beliefs mentioned

A Is for Abigail: An Almanac of Amazing American Women (U.S.)
Lynne Cheney; illustrated by Robin Preiss Glasser

Proceeding through the alphabet, *A Is for Abigail* honors the women who helped shape America. Bold, colorful illustrations with plenty of interesting tidbits and facts on each page make this a compelling read as you investigate U.S. history with your children. I learned so much!

A Is for Aloha: A Hawai'i Alphabet (U.S.)
U'ilani Goldsberry; illustrated by Tammy Yee

This introduction to Hawaii provides a wealth of details about the islands' culture. An overview of the languages, customs, and history makes me want to board the next flight to one of my favorite places. *Note: Religious beliefs mentioned*

American Tall Tales (U.S.)
Mary Pope Osborne; illustrated by Michael McCurdy

This revised collection of tall tales features the typical inclusions of Pecos Bill, Johnny Appleseed, Davy Crockett, and Paul Bunyan as well as new stories about Stormalong, Febold Feboldson, and Thunder Ann Whirlwind. Fun for read-alouds and to deepen your children's understanding of these legendary figures.

And Then What Happened, Paul Revere? (U.S.)
Jean Fritz; illustrated by Margot Tomes

This historical retelling includes lesser known details about the patriot (such as his stint silversmithing for squirrels!) and also highlights the events leading up to his famous ride. Make sure you check out Fritz's other U.S. history titles: *Shh! We're Writing the Constitution*; *Can't You Make Them Behave, King George?*; *What's the Big Idea, Ben Franklin?*; *Will You Sign Here, John Hancock?*; and more.

Baseball Saved Us (Japan/U.S.)
Ken Mochizuki; illustrated by Dom Lee

"Shorty" and his Japanese-American family have been sent to an internment camp after the attack on Pearl Harbor. Despite their humiliation and the racism they suffer, they form a baseball league as a distraction for the camp's residents. Shorty doesn't usually play well, but in one game he channels all his anger into the swing and scores a home run.

The Bracelet (Japan/U.S.) | Yoshiko Uchida

Emi must pack away her dolls and books—her family has been ordered to report to a Japanese internment camp. Her friend, Laurie, shows up at the door with a goodbye gift, a gold bracelet, and Emi promises to never take it off. But when the bracelet goes missing, Emi discovers that what she holds close in her heart no one can ever steal.

The Childhood of Famous Americans Series (U.S.)

With over seventy titles (and still counting!), this series of fictionalized biographies introduces young readers to noteworthy Americans, specifically focusing on what they were like as kids *before* becoming well-known figures. Includes presidents, sports stars, authors, TV personalities, and more. My children enjoy these (and I've been known to get caught up in them myself!).

The Children's Book of America (U.S.)
William Bennett; illustrated by Michael Hague

The kids and I stumbled upon this inspiring title at our local library and have appreciated its collection of songs, poems, and classic retellings of U.S. history. Our favorite passages include the segments on Abigail Adams, Lewis and Clark, and "The Star-Spangled Banner."

The Courage of Sarah Noble (U.S.)
Alice Dalgliesh—Newbery Honor

Sarah Noble has said goodbye to her mother and siblings to start a new life for the family in Connecticut with her father. Her mother's parting refrain to "Keep up your courage" stays with the eight-year-old through the uncertain times that follow: encounters with wolves, Native Americans, and being separated from her father. This inspiring true story takes place just half an hour from our home!

The First Thanksgiving (U.S.)
Jean Craighead George; illustrated by Thomas Locker

Thomas Locker's watercolor paintings beautifully enhance this rendition of the Thanksgiving story. The book traces the passage of time from the creation of Plymouth Rock to the final celebration between Pilgrims and Native Americans.

If You Lived at the Time of the American Revolution (U.S.)
Kay Moore; Daniel O'Leary

What was it like to live, work, and learn during the American Revolution? This title explores interesting questions and answers, like the perspective of Loyalists and the role that children played in this historical period. Keep an eye out for other titles in the If You Lived Series, including *If You Lived in Colonial Times*, *If You Lived at the Time of the Civil War*, *If You Were There When They Signed the Constitution*, *If You Traveled on the Underground Railroad*, and more.

How Many Days to America?: A Thanksgiving Story (U.S.)
Eve Bunting; illustrated by Beth Peck

After soldiers show up at their door, a family from the Caribbean sets sail at night for freedom in the United States. They face harrowing, dangerous conditions in a small boat on the sea until they land on Thanksgiving Day, their freedom finally secure.

May B. (U.S.) | Caroline Starr Rose

May has reluctantly agreed to help on a stranger's homestead for a few months, but soon she finds herself unexpectedly stranded—alone—with winter approaching. Her courage to survive and return home ultimately gives her the confidence to overcome even her greatest challenge: reading. A beautiful novel in verse—perfect for *Little House* lovers and those dealing with dyslexia or other learning disabilities.

GLOBAL PERSPECTIVE

How do you give your children the world in your home?

"A homeschool postcard swap group allows us to 'meet' other homeschool families throughout the world, and we try to take advantage of all the traveling cultural performances/events in our city: concerts, dance, art exhibits, festivals, etc." Catherine, Tennessee

Ultimate U.S. Road Trip Atlas (U.S.) | National Geographic

This atlas is far too interesting to save just for road trips! A two-page spread features a map of each state along with cool things to do there, fast facts, and random laws that you have to read to believe. Jonathan spent hours in his room with this title—coming out multiple times to update me with the amazing tidbits he had learned.

The New Americans: Colonial Times: 1620–1689 (U.S.)
Betsy Maestro; illustrated by Giulio Maestro

Part of an ongoing series about the nation's early history, this installment covers the settlement by the Pilgrims, their relationships with the Native Americans, the desire for religious freedom, and more. Interesting watercolors and maps balanced with just the right amount of text will hold the attention of young scholars. If your kids like this one, check out the others by the same author. *Note: Some illustrations depict bloodshed and battle.*

Our 50 States: A Family Adventure Across America (U.S.)
Lynne Cheney; illustrated by Robin Preiss Glasser

Pack your bags for an ultimate road trip through all fifty states alongside the family of five in this book. Each state is featured on one or two pages with important facts, dates, and interesting trivia the kids in the road-tripping family discover throughout their trip.

Phoebe the Spy (U.S.) | Judith Griffin; illustrated by Margot Tomes
Who is planning to kill George Washington? An unlikely spy, thirteen-year-old Phoebe Fraunces must find out. Posing as Washington's housekeeper, the girl keeps her eyes and ears wide open to report any suspicious activity—before it's too late.

Ten Mile Day: And the Building of the Transcontinental Railroad (U.S.)
Mary Ann Fraser

It had been said that railroad tracks could never completely stretch from east to west, but this day proved the naysayers wrong. Thoroughly researched and beautifully illustrated, Fraser describes the moment the final tracks were laid—and the ten-thousand-dollar wager that drove the men on to see if they could lay a record of ten miles in one day.

That Book Woman (U.S.)
Heather Hensen; illustrated by David Small

Cal lives high in the Appalachian Mountains, where he works hard with his Pap and doesn't have time for anything else, especially reading. Slowly, though, someone changes his mind—the courageous "book woman" who makes the trek to their house with a lending library. Based on the true story of the Pack Horse Librarians in the 1930s.

The Wall (U.S.) | Eve Bunting; illustrated by Ronald Himler

This moving story follows the pilgrimage of a young boy and his father to the Vietnam Veterans Memorial in Washington, D.C., as they search for the name of the boy's grandpa. The combination of soul-stirring words and illustrations naturally leads to an opportunity to discuss war and grief.

We the People: The Story of Our Constitution (U.S.)
Lynne Cheney; illustrated by Greg Harlin

America had won the Revolution, but we were far from united. In this post-war time of debt, insecurity, and squabbling between states, delegates gather to piece together a new set of governing guidelines—the Constitution. A fascinating read filled with plenty of facts and quotes from the Founding Fathers.

When Jessie Came Across the Sea (U.S.)
Amy Hest; illustrated by P. J. Lynch

Thirteen-year-old Jessie has received the chance of a lifetime: a free ticket on a ship headed to America. But stepping on board means saying goodbye to the only family she has: her grandmother. Jessie bravely crosses the Atlantic with the hope that one day her grandmother will join her.

Who Was/What Was Series (U.S.)

This growing series encompasses over one hundred biographies of individuals in both U.S. and world history. From figures like Harriet Tubman, Helen Keller, and Clara Barton to past presidents and beyond, these short biographies include enticing, cartoon-like illustrations as well as interesting facts. Also check out the corresponding What Was? Series with titles about the Statue of Liberty, Boston Tea Party, March on Washington, and more. Trishna has read a dozen of these and always asks for another!

NORTH AMERICAN BOOKS FOR AGES 10-12

Ashley Bryan: Words to My Life's Song (African American)
Ashley Bryan

Well-known children's book illustrator Ashley Bryan grew up poor, but that didn't stop him from creating. His parents noticed his gift and bought a desk for his work and supplies. Looking back over his life, Bryan tells readers how the Bible inspired him, how racism tried to block his way, and how he found the courage to keep sharing his art with the world. *Note: Christian beliefs mentioned*

Bad News for Outlaws: The Remarkable Life of Bass Reeves, Deputy U.S. Marshal (African American)
Vaunda Micheaux Nelson; illustrated by R. Gregory Christie

Bass Reeves escaped a life of slavery and ended up in Indian Territory, ultimately becoming the first African American U.S. Marshal. Reeves had his work cut out for him during this unsettled, dangerous time in the country's history, and his boldness and bravery made him a legend in the Old West. Suspenseful and dramatic!

Christmas in the Big House, Christmas in the Quarters (African American) | Patricia C. McKissack; illustrated by John Thompson

After discovering this title, I immediately ordered a copy to add to our holiday book collection. Full of carefully researched details, it illuminates the stark contrast between Christmas for the master's family and Christmas for slaves on a Virginian plantation in 1859. Realistic illustrations combine with narrative, songs, recipes, and poems, bringing to life the period before the Civil War.

Elijah of Buxton (African American)
Christopher Paul Curtis—Newbery Honor

Eleven-year-old Elijah is the first child born free in the new settlement of Buxton, Canada. But the quest for liberty isn't over yet, as the timid boy learns when funds saved to free another family suddenly go missing. Elijah's pursuit of the money takes him back to the United States where he sees slavery firsthand, risks his life, and grows into a brave young man. *Note: The topics dealt with in this novel make it a good read-aloud, opening the door to deep family discussions*

GLOBAL PERSPECTIVE

How do you give your children the world in your home?

"I am passionate about passing on to my kids a global perspective. God has made so many different people and cultures, and I want them to be able to converse and feel comfortable with a variety of people. We support a missionary and have some children in India and Haiti we also support. We are able to write letters to them." Jaime, Canada

Anne of Green Gables (Canada) | L. M. Montgomery

I debated not including Anne with an *e* here, not because she doesn't belong but because many of you know her already. Yet putting together a Canadian book list without her feels a bit like making chocolate cake without the chocolate. If you've never had the chance to meet the redheaded orphan who mistakenly comes to live with the Cuthberts, read it yourself and then share it with your tween or teen! Keep an eye out for the other books in the *Anne* series as well as Montgomery's other novels—all of which paint a lovely portrait of Prince Edward Island and other areas of Canada.

The Snake Scientist (Canada)
Sy Montgomery; photographs by Nic Bishop

In this exciting choice for budding scientists, Sy Montgomery follows a well-known snake expert to the Canadian prairie, where thousands of garter snakes turn up each spring after hibernation. A passion for nature and preservation wriggles across each page as the researchers pick up fistfuls of snakes to study, trying to figure out the unsolved mysteries of the creatures.

Blue Birds (Native American) | Caroline Starr Rose

Tensions between the Roanoke and the English have been rising long before twelve-year-old Alis steps onto shore. That doesn't stop her, however, from forming a secret bond with Kimi, a Roanoke girl she meets in the woods. As conflicts mount between their two sides, the girls must choose where their loyalties lie. A gripping novel-in-verse about friendship, family, and the people we now call the Lost Colony. *Note: Native American religious beliefs mentioned*

Island of the Blue Dolphins (Native American)
Scott O'Dell—Newbery Medal

Historians believe that during the 1800s a Native American girl camped on a Pacific island alone for eighteen years after jumping from a rescue boat while attempting to save her little brother. This is her story—of survival, of love for nature, and of courage. *Note: Native American religious beliefs mentioned*

Sing Down the Moon (Native American)
Scott O' Dell—Newbery Honor

Fourteen-year-old Bright Morning and her friend Running Bird have taken the sheep out to pasture on a lovely spring morning. It's a typical day—until they see Spanish slavers riding toward them. Sold to wealthy women, the girls begin to plan their escape. An introduction to the Navajo's forced march to Fort Sumner. *Note: Native American religious beliefs mentioned*

Children of the Dust Bowl: The True Story of the School at Weedpatch Camp (U.S.) | Jerry Stanley

"When a farmer couldn't pay the bank, a tractor was sent to knock down his farmhouse as a way of forcing him to leave the land." During the 1930s, thousands of families from Oklahoma left for the promised land of California, only to find an even harsher poverty than they had previously known. The farmers' children go without school until a local superintendent and the kids create their own.

Factory Girl (U.S.) | Barbara Greenwood

Twelve-year-old Emily dreams of completing the eighth grade and becoming a nurse, clerk, or teacher. But when her father, who went west seeking work, stops sending checks, Emily knows she must keep the family from starving. Her journey into child labor leads to the Acme Garment Factory, where she works eleven hours a day clipping loose threads in terrible conditions. An eye-opening work of historical fiction.

Immigrant Kids (U.S.) | Russell Freedman

If your family had recently arrived at Ellis Island, what would your life as a kid be like—at home, at school, at work, at play? Newbery Medal–winning author Russell Freedman shows us in this book, combining vintage photos with descriptions from children themselves. Insightful and real.

Johnny Tremain (U.S.) | Esther Hoskins Forbes—Newbery Medal

Fourteen-year-old Johnny excels in his work as a silversmith until a tragic accident prematurely ends his apprenticeship. Depressed and alone, he stumbles into another job in Boston that leads him straight to the Patriots, the Boston Tea Party, and the Battle of Lexington. Suspenseful!

Journey to Topaz: A Story of the Japanese-American Evacuation (Japan/U.S.) | Yoshiko Uchida; illustrated by Donald Carrick

Yuki has the hopes and cares of most eleven-year-olds: Christmas around the corner, taking care of pets, dealing with her teasing brother. But in an instant, everything changes with the radio report about Pearl Harbor. Soon Father is sent away and later they all must leave home. Though historical fiction, the author pulls heavily from her own experience in this moving account. Uchida writes about being set free from the camp in her sequel, *Journey Home.*

The Perilous Road (U.S.) | William O. Steele—Newbery Honor

Born and bred in Tennessee, Chris can't stand Yankees. They stole his father's horses and crops and deserve to be punished. So when the boy sees their wagon train on the road, he reports it—only to find out later that his brother is one of the drivers. Desperate to warn him about the impending attack, Chris rushes through the Yankee camps and discovers a surprising truth—they aren't monsters after all.

GLOBAL PERSPECTIVE

How do you give your children the world in your home?

"When we moved houses, we intentionally sought out a more ethnically and racially diverse neighborhood. Even though our new neighborhood is only a few miles away, we are surrounded by rich diversity and we encounter people from all walks of life in our daily interactions at the market and the park. This has expanded our social circle and allowed my children to make friends with people who have different backgrounds. It has been an enriching gift for our whole family." Erika, California

Shades of Gray (U.S.) | Carolyn Reeder

Will's entire family died as a result of the Civil War. Now that the war is over, he must live with unknown relatives, including his Uncle Jed who refused to fight the Yankees. Will can't stand the thought of staying with a coward and traitor, but as time passes, he finds out that courage isn't always black-and-white.

Sylvia & Aki (U.S.) | Winifred Conkling

Sylvia and Aki don't know it yet, but they have something in common: both are victims of injustice. Aki has been sent away from her family's farm to an internment camp. Sylvia's family now rents Aki's farm but she can't attend the local school, which closes its doors to Mexicans. The novel goes on to describe the landmark court case, brought by Sylvia's father, which led to the desegregation of schools for Latino children.

Toliver's Secret (U.S.) | Esther Wood Brady

Ellen can't believe that her grandfather spies for the Patriots, but she gets an even bigger surprise when he asks her to take over his dangerous mission! Disguised as a boy, the ten-year-old must deliver a loaf of bread with a secret message inside for George Washington. Can she overcome the dangers and obstacles to reach the general safely?

CHAPTER 11

A HARVEST OF HOPE: LATIN AMERICA

Countries/regions included in this chapter: Brazil, Caribbean, Chile, Colombia, Costa Rica, Cuba, Ecuador, French Guiana, Guatemala, Haiti, Honduras, Jamaica, Mexico, Nicaragua, Panama, Peru, Puerto Rico, Venezuela

Not too long ago, a friend told me about an app that will teach you foreign languages for free. I excitedly downloaded it on my phone to brush up on years of forgotten Spanish. I fit the engaging, short lessons in here and there— while waiting in the car, during a quiet afternoon, or when hanging out after dinner with the family. A few weeks later, an inspired Jonathan asked, "Could I start learning Spanish, too?" What mama could refuse?

When you study a language, you naturally find yourself interested in that part of the world as well. Lucky for us I had *Give Your Child the World* research keeping me busy. I was bringing many books on this list home from the library to read myself and pass on to the kids. I'm sure you'll discover some family favorites here—and maybe learning about Latin America will lead to foreign-language study in your neck of the woods too!

LATIN AMERICAN BOOKS FOR AGES 4–6

The Rainforest Grew All Around (Brazil)
Susan Mitchell; illustrated by Connie McLennan

On these pages, a familiar childhood rhythm ("The Green Grass Grows All Around") takes on new lyrics that introduce little ones to the ecosystems of the rain forest. It includes activities to complete in the back of the book as well as a recipe using ingredients from the region.

My Little Island (Caribbean) | Frané Lessac

A beautiful overview of island living, this sweet book traces the journey of a young boy visiting the Caribbean country where he was born. I love the colorful illustrations that showcase his family's vibrant island lifestyle.

Biblioburro: A True Story from Colombia (Colombia)
Jeanette Winter

Luis adores books and that's the problem—his house overflows with them, and his wife says they have to go. Suddenly, he has an idea: What if he took the books over the mountains where the children don't have any? Luis faces bandits and plenty of challenges along the way, but he finally makes it to the faraway village for a unique story hour.

The Umbrella (Costa Rica) | Jan Brett

Carlos makes an umbrella to keep himself dry as he searches for rain-forest animals. To get a better view he climbs a tree, leaving his leafy umbrella alone at the bottom. Little does he know that one by one the animals he's hoping to see find his discarded umbrella and hop aboard. Love!

The Bossy Gallito: A Traditional Cuban Folktale (Cuba)
Lucia M. Gonzalez; illustrated by Lulu Delacre

In this bilingual folktale, a greedy rooster is on his way to his uncle's wedding. He dirties his beak while eating and tries unsuccessfully to get himself clean again, until some assistance from the sun helps him look his best. A silly read-aloud!

We're Sailing to Galapagos: A Week in the Pacific (Ecuador)
Laurie Krebs; illustrated by Grazia Restelli

This colorful, rhyming book introduces young listeners to the animals of the Galapagos Islands. An appendix includes more details about the creatures for slightly older children. Fun illustrations!

Arroz con Leche: Popular Songs and Rhymes from Latin America (Latin America) | Lulu Delacre

Arroz con Leche contains songs, poems, and kid-friendly games in both English and Spanish. The artwork beautifully personifies childhood in Latin America.

GLOBAL PERSPECTIVE

How do you give your children the world in your home?

"We have always prayed for missionaries around the world and studied where they lived, but now we are living in Brazil as missionaries and seeing the reality that life is very different in other places. Our children are immersed in a culture that is not their own. We now read about other parts of the world with a new perspective." Charlotte, Brazil

New Shoes for Silvia (Latin America)
Johanna Hurwitz; illustrated by Jerry Pinkney

Silvia's aunt sent her a pair of new red shoes, but they are too big. While waiting impatiently to grow into them, she plays with the shoes in other ways—turning them into a doll bed, a train, and oxen in a field. Weeks pass and Silvia moves on to other pursuits, only to stumble upon the pair and find out they finally fit!

Papa and Me (Latin America)
Arthur Dorros; illustrated by Rudy Guitierrez

A young boy wakes with excitement, knowing he gets to spend the whole day with his papa. Going about their ordinary routine, the father and son complete their tasks in a way that highlights their love for one another. Features some Spanish words and phrases along with their translations.

¡Pío Peep!: Traditional Spanish Nursery Rhymes (Latin America)
Edited by Alma Flor Ada, F. Isabel Campoy & Alice Schertle; illustrated by Vivi Escriva

This is a delightful collection of bilingual nursery rhymes—including poems, fingerplays, and games—paired with charming watercolors. A lovely first look at Latin American culture for little ones.

Abuela (Mexico/U.S.) | Arthur Dorros; illustrated by Elisa Kleven
Abuela and her granddaughter feed the birds in the park, leading to an imaginative flight high over New York City. Rosalba and her grandmother take in and

describe the sights in both Spanish and English phrases, many of which remind Abuela of what it was like when she first arrived in the country.

The Cazuela That the Farm Maiden Stirred (Mexico)
Samantha R. Vamos; illustrated by Rafael Lopez

Building on the familiar cadence of "The House That Jack Built," this silly tale describes the day a farm maiden forgets the dish cooking in her pot and needs help from several farm animals to save it. The pages slowly introduce Spanish vocabulary and conclude with a recipe for the *arroz con leche* that the maiden creates.

Off We Go to Mexico (Mexico)
Laurie Krebs; illustrated by Christopher Corr

Discover Mexican culture alongside a family traveling via canyon train to explore some of the country's most well-known symbols. Little ones will enjoy the rhyming text, brightly colored drawings, and the Spanish words introduced on each page. *Note: Religious beliefs briefly mentioned*

The Tortilla Factory (Mexico)
Gary Paulsen; illustrated by Ruth Wright Paulsen

Follow the making of a tortilla by watching the men and women who create them—from seed to corn to flour to oven. The cycle continues as the workers eat the tortillas, giving them strength to plant the seeds and keep their efforts going. Gorgeous paintings convey the culture and allow readers to fully imagine the process.

What Can You Do with a Paleta? (Mexico)
Carmen Tafolla; illustrated by Magaly Morales

This colorful story familiarizes young readers with the icy popsicle Mexican children love—the paleta! A young girl describes her favorite delicacy and her barrio as she strolls through it while licking her melting treat. Also check out *What Can You Do with a Rebozo?* by the same author.

Conejito: A Folktale from Panama (Panama)
Margaret Read MacDonald; illustrated by Geraldo Valerio

Conejito, a young rabbit on school holiday, goes to visit his Aunt Tia. She stuffs him full of cakes and goodies that he enjoys, but on the way home he finds that

Fox, Tiger, and Lion want a treat too! Youngsters will laugh out loud at this retelling of a Central American folktale.

Moon Rope/Un lazo a la luna (Peru) | Lois Ehlert

In this bilingual Peruvian story, we follow Fox and Mole as they go to the moon. Fox succeeds in making it to their destination, but Mole gets nervous and falls. To this day, moles hide in underground tunnels to avoid their embarrassment. Ancient Peruvian textiles and ceramics inspire *Moon Rope's* bold illustrations.

Juan Bobo Goes to Work: A Puerto Rican Folktale (Puerto Rico)
Marisa Montes; illustrated by Jose Cepeda

Foolish Juan Bobo tries to do as he's told, but he can't seem to stay out of mischief. After payment for a job falls through a hole in his pocket, his mother tells him to put his next wages in a burlap sack. Unfortunately, he receives milk as his next payment. This cycle continues until his silliness brings good luck to the family after all.

LATIN AMERICAN BOOKS FOR AGES 6-8

Cassio's Day: From Dawn to Dusk in a Brazilian Village (Brazil)
Maria de Fatima Campos

Come take in the sights as six-year-old Cassio walks us through each step of his family's routine—offering us a glimpse of daily Brazilian life. Photographs, Portuguese words, and a glossary combine into a comprehensive look at this country. Also check out the others in the series: *Yikang's Day* (China), *Nii Kwei's Day* (Ghana), *Geeta's Day* (India), *Bongani's Day* (South Africa), *Enrique's Day* (Peru), *Polina's Day* (Russia), *Boushra's Day* (Egypt), and *Iina-Marja's Day* (Arctic). *Note: Religious beliefs mentioned*

The Great Kapok Tree: A Tale of the Amazon Rain Forest (Brazil)
Lynne Cherry

A laborer arrives in the forest with his axe, determined to chop down a large kapok tree. After working for a while he pauses to rest, falling asleep beneath it. One by one, the animals that live there whisper to him why their tree should live. When the man wakes, he realizes he's had a change of heart.

Victoria Goes to Brazil (Brazil) | Maria de Fatima Campos

Victoria lives with her Brazilian mother in London, and during her school holidays they venture across the ocean for a visit. The girl offers readers her first impressions on the busy city of Sao Paulo, the relatives and friends she meets, and the food that differs from what she eats back home. *Note: Catholic beliefs mentioned*

My Grandpa and the Sea (Caribbean) | Katherine Orr

Grandpa loves the sea and makes his living with his small fishing boat. But developing technologies deplete his supply of fish. Discouraged but determined, Grandpa comes up with a new type of crop—sea moss, which enables him to continue his work. *Note: Mentions that Grandpa does not go to church but meets with God on the sea*

My Name Is Gabriela (Chile)
Monica Brown; illustrated by John Parra

Come meet the first Latina woman to win the Nobel Prize for Literature—Gabriela Mistral. As a girl, Gabriela falls in love with words, poetry, and education. She spends the rest of her life perfecting her craft and teaching others. An inspiring, bilingual picture book.

GLOBAL PERSPECTIVE

How do you give your children the world in your home?

"My girls were born in Colombia so on every 'Family Day' we give them a gift from or about that country, often a book. We are also blessed to live in a culturally diverse city with lots of restaurants, and several of our friends are missionaries all over the world." Penny, Ohio

Waiting for the Biblioburro (Colombia)
Monica Brown; illustrated by John Parra

Ana reads the one and only book she owns over and over. Her teacher gave it to her before moving away. Now there's no one to teach the village's children, until a man shows up with books strapped to two donkeys. Ana's dreams to learn come true as she continues to read—and receives encouragement to write her own story.

Fernando's Gift (Costa Rica) | Douglas Keister

Fernando and his family live deep within the Costa Rican rain forest. He loves climbing trees and playing outside with his best friend, Carmina. But one day Carmina discovers her favorite tree has been chopped down by those who don't share the same respect Carmina and Fernando have for their land. What can Fernando do to help?

The Forest in the Clouds (Costa Rica)
Sneed B. Collard; illustrated by Michael Rothman

Come visit the Monte Verde cloud forest—a unique ecosystem high in the mountains of the rain forest. Meet the interesting plants, insects, and animals that thrive in this landscape and learn the steps being taken to protect their home.

The Forever Forest: Kids Save a Tropical Treasure (Costa Rica)
Kristin Joy Pratt-Serafini & Rachel Crandell

Peter travels with his mother from Sweden to Costa Rica on a visit to the "Forever Forest." As they learn about the creatures that live there, he's surprised to discover that twenty years ago kids from around the world raised money to protect the property—and that his mother was one of the children who started it all.

A Little Book of Sloth (Costa Rica) | Lucy Cooke

Animal lovers in your home will get a kick out of these sloths, who have been photographed in their Costa Rican sanctuary. Besides the cute factor (a warning on the back cover states that "baby sloths can be highly addictive"), the book informs readers about these unique animals and the place in which they live.

Roses for Isabella (Ecuador)
Diana Cohn; illustrated by Neil Waldman

Isabella's parents once worked on a rose farm that used unhealthy chemicals, which made her mother sick. Now the girl is grateful to work on land that grows flowers using eco-friendly methods. The young girl writes a poem about the beautiful farm and reads it at a village ceremony honoring the earth. Introduces the concept of fair trade. *Note: Tribal religious beliefs mentioned*

Abuela's Weave (Guatemala)
Omar S. Castaneda; illustrated by Enrique Sanchez

Guatemalan culture comes alive in this tale of a girl and her grandmother. The two weave beautiful tapestries to sell in the local market. But machine-made tapestries have now become popular, and they wonder if the villagers will still want their creations.

Guatemala ABCs: A Book about the People and Places of Guatemala (Guatemala) | Marcie Aboff; illustrated by Zachary Le Trover

This book presents both common and lesser-known details about Guatemalan culture in an alphabetical format. Entries cover animals, plants, history, and people groups. *Note: Catholic and Mayan religious beliefs mentioned*

Tap-Tap (Haiti) | Karen Lynn Williams; illustrated by Catherine Stock

For the first time, eight-year-old Sasifi joins her mother to sell oranges at the village market. Tired on the hot journey, the girl longs to ride in a tap-tap, a Haitian truck that passes them by. After working hard all day, Sasifi finally gets her wish. Colorful watercolors bring Haiti to life for young readers.

Anansi the Spider Man (Jamaica)
Philip M. Sherlock; illustrated by Marcia Brown

The stars of this collection of short stories, originally published in 1954, are Anansi the Spider Man and the many tricks he plays on other island animals. Features charmingly simple pen and ink drawings.

The Gold Coin (Latin America)
Alma Flor Ada; illustrated by Neil Waldman

When Juan, the village thief, overhears Doña Josefa talking about her gold coin, he makes plans to steal it. He soon discovers, however, that the woman isn't just an old lady, but a transformational force in her community. After watching her for several days, Juan changes his mind . . . and his life. Heartwarming—one of my favorites!

A Mango in the Hand: A Story Told Through Proverbs (Latin America)
Antonio Sacre; illustrated by Sebastia Serra

It's Francisco's saint day, and his father says he's old enough to collect mangoes from the tree by himself. His dad continues offering advice, in the form of wise proverbs, as the boy faces one obstacle after another, determined to persevere and bring home dessert. *Note: Catholic beliefs mentioned*

Borreguita and the Coyote (Mexico)
Verna Aardema; illustrated by Petra Mathers

In this traditional folktale, a clever lamb outwits a not-so-clever coyote that wants to eat her. This classic trickster story will make readers laugh out loud, and the illustrations of the Mexican countryside are a lovely bonus.

Diego Rivera: His World and Ours (Mexico) | Duncan Tonatiuh

Have any budding artists at home? They'll enjoy this introduction to artist Diego Rivera, which includes details of his mischievous childhood adventures and how he discovered painting. Using Diego's work as a teaching tool, the text also presents common artistic styles and terms. *Note: Traditional Mayan beliefs briefly mentioned*

GLOBAL PERSPECTIVE

How do you give your children the world in your home?

"We spent five years in the U.S., where we met tons of different people. We've taught our children to have an open mind to other countries by reading books or telling them about countries we visited before they were born. Next year, we will start traveling around the world for our summer break. We are from France, but part of my family is in Mexico, our next destination!" Marie, France

Elena's Serenade (Mexico) | Campbell Geeslin; illustrated by Ana Juan
Elena wants to be a glassblower like her father, but he tells her girls can't do the job. She sets out to prove him wrong, taking a trip disguised as a boy to nearby

Monterrey where the best glassblowers live. A fanciful, childlike story full of spunk and a bit of magic too.

Gathering the Sun: An Alphabet in Spanish and English (Mexico/U.S.)
Alma Flor Ada; illustrated by Simon Silva

With rich illustrations that highlight Mexican-American culture, *Gathering the Sun* proceeds through each letter of the Spanish alphabet, accompanied by a bilingual poem. The beauty of working the land and bringing in its harvest shines through each page—gorgeous!

Hill of Fire (Mexico) | Thomas P. Lewis; illustrated by Joan Sandin

Pablo's father feels that each day is the same—nothing interesting ever happens in their village. That changes the day his cornfield begins to hiss and spew out smoke. A nearby volcano is erupting and the family must flee. Based on a true story from 1943.

The Legend of the Poinsettia (Mexico) | Tomie dePaola

Lucida wants to offer a gift to the baby Jesus at Christmas, but having ruined a newly made blanket, she stumbles toward the church empty-handed. A kind old woman encourages her to give what she has, so the girl gathers a few weeds in her arms. When she places them in the manger, a miracle occurs. *Note: Christian beliefs mentioned*

The Moon Was at a Fiesta (Mexico)
Matthew Gollub; illustrated by Leovigildo Martinez

For years, the sun and moon happily maintained their own separate hours. But when the moon hears about parties during the day, she jealously decides to host her own fiesta and the trouble begins. This original folktale explains why the moon sometimes appears during the day.

Nine Days to Christmas (Mexico)
Marie Hall Ets & Aurora Labastida—Caldecott Medal

Ceci is now old enough to join her village in its Christmas posadas—the Mexican processions that reenact the Christmas story. There will be friends, food, a piñata, and a bit of holiday magic. This delightful story made me think of the Velveteen Rabbit!

My Papa Diego and Me: Memories of My Father and His Art (Mexico)
Guadalupe Rivera Marin

Guadalupe Marin, daughter of artist Diego Rivera, created this book as a tribute to her father. Using fourteen of his most famous paintings as a guide, she explains his love for children, his passion for education, and what it was like growing up in Mexico.

The Piñata Maker (Mexico) | George Ancona

This bilingual title blends photographs with words to teach readers the art of piñata making. A young boy begins by delivering materials to Tio Rico, the older man in the community known for his piñatas. It follows him through each step in the process, including a children's party where one of his creations is opened. Fun!

The Pot That Juan Built (Mexico)
Nancy Andrews-Goebel; illustrated by David Diaz

This cumulative tale acquaints listeners with Mexican potter Juan Quezada, a man who rediscovers an ancient way to create beautiful pottery and thereby revitalizes an entire village. One side of the page presents the rhyming text as it slowly builds on itself, while the other offers extra real-life details that may interest slightly older readers.

Tomas and the Library Lady (Mexico/U.S.)
Pat Mora; illustrated by Raul Colon

Tomas, the son of migrant workers, must leave his beloved home in Texas to follow the work and the harvest in Iowa. But the "library lady" helps him forget his homesickness and opens a magical world to the boy—one that he passes on to his family and that changes his entire life. This true story brought tears to my eyes!

Too Many Tamales (Mexico/U.S.)
Gary Soto; illustrated by Ed Martinez

Maria is excited about helping Mother make traditional tamales on this magical Christmas Eve, complete with falling snow. If only she can try on her mom's diamond ring while she works, the night will be perfect. When the ring disappears later, the children gather to search for it—leading to a lot of eating and way too many tamales!

Uncle Nacho's Hat (Nicaragua)
Harriet Rohmer; illustrated by Veg Reisberg

Uncle Nacho just can't seem to part with his old hat. Even when his niece gives him a new one, the man struggles to leave the past behind. A comical Nicaraguan folktale kids will enjoy about coming to terms with change.

Tonight Is Carnaval (Peru) | Arthur Dorros

A Peruvian boy and his family excitedly prepare for the upcoming festival of Carnaval. I love these illustrations, which represent traditional fabric wall hangings called *arpilleras*. An afterword includes details about how arpilleras are made.

Roberto's Trip to the Top (Venezuela)
John B. Paterson Jr.; illustrated by John B. Paterson Sr.

Roberto excitedly heads up the mountain via cable car with his Uncle Antonio, hovering high above the city of Caracas. With a new camera, he captures everything for his papa, until at the top he accidentally drops it into a ravine. Disappointed, the boy must find another way to document his special day.

LATIN AMERICAN BOOKS FOR AGES 8-10

The Great Snake: Stories from the Amazon (Brazil)
Sean Taylor; illustrated by Fernando Vilela

This gripping introduction to nine legends of the rain forest paired with brightly colored drawings entertains readers with stories of cobras, jaguars, villagers, and mystery. Includes a glossary with notes about the region. *Note: Religious beliefs mentioned*

The Most Beautiful Place in the World (Guatemala) | Ann Cameron

After his new stepfather rejects him, Juan lives in poverty with his grandmother. He must take to the street shining shoes in order to bring in money for them, but his greatest desire is to go to school. Will Grandmother agree?

Eight Days: A Story of Haiti (Haiti)
Edwidge Danticat; illustrated by Alix Delinois

This picture book finds its roots in the true story of a seven-year-old survivor of Haiti's 2010 earthquake. When rescuers found the boy after eight days under a house, they asked him if he was afraid. He answered, "I missed my family . . . in my mind, I played." Touching, sad, and joyful.

The Good Garden: How One Family Went from Hunger to Having Enough (Honduras) | Katie Smith Milway; illustrated by Sylvie Daigneault

Maria's family works the land as farmers, but they never have enough after dealing with a middleman who exploits their efforts. Then a new teacher comes to the community and demonstrates sustainable farming techniques that allow them to cut out the middleman altogether. A moving story.

Come Look with Me, Latin American Art (Latin America)
Kimberly Lane

This installment in a popular series features a dozen paintings from Latin American artists. Each two-page spread includes background information on the artists, their culture, and the style of their work. Questions to readers allow them to use their own imaginations as they study the images.

Armando and the Blue Tarp School (Mexico) | Edith Hope Fine & Judith Pinkerton Josephson; illustrated by Hernan Sosa

Armando lives on a trash dump and spends his days picking through garbage for anything to use or sell. But when a man shows up with a blue tarp and begins to teach the local children, the boy's parents allow him to join in—knowing that education leads to a better life. Based on a remarkable true story.

Harvesting Hope: The Story of Cesar Chavez (Mexico/U.S.)
Kathleen Krull; illustrated by Yuyi Morales

A severe drought has forced Cesar Chavez's family to leave their farm in Arizona and become Californian migrant workers. In the fields, the boy comes face-to-face with injustice and oppression. As a young man, his bold choice to organize a march and strike leads to the first contract with farm workers in America—all accomplished without violence. Inspiring!

In My Family/En mi familia (Mexico) | Carmen Lomas Garza

This beautiful book features thirteen of Garza's paintings alongside descriptions of common Mexican-American traditions in both English and Spanish. Also check out *Family Pictures* by the same author/artist. *Note: Religious beliefs mentioned*

My Diary from Here to There (Mexico)
Amada Irma Perez; illustrated by Maya Christina Gonzalez

After being tucked into bed one night, Amada overhears her parents discussing a move from Mexico to Los Angeles. She worries about leaving her country, learning another language, and discovering a new way of life, but as their journey progresses, she finds that what her father says is true: she is "stronger than she thinks."

Lost City: The Discovery of Machu Picchu (Peru) | Ted Lewin

Follow explorer Hiram Bingham in the year 1911 and imagine what it was like to discover the ruins of Machu Picchu! This book is both a fascinating historical account and a story of perseverance that pays off.

Martin de Porres: The Rose in the Desert (Peru)
Gary D. Schmidt; illustrated by David Diaz

Martin, the son of a former slave and a Spanish nobleman, leads a life marked by constant poverty. In spite of his disadvantages, the boy grows up wanting to serve others. Told he can never be a priest because of his race, he joins the monastery as a servant instead. After decades of faithful work, Martin de Porres becomes the first black saint in the Americas. *Note: Catholic beliefs mentioned*

My Name Is Maria Isabel (Puerto Rico)
Alma Flor Ada; illustrated by K. Dyble Thompson

A young girl wants to be called by her proper name—Maria. It's a simple request, yet when she arrives at a new school, there are already two Marias in her class. Her teacher suggests she goes by "Mary" instead. But Maria continually forgets to respond to the name, until an essay assignment gives her an outlet to share her feelings.

LATIN AMERICAN BOOKS FOR AGES 10–12

Journey to the River Sea (Brazil) | Eva Ibbotson

Maia's parents died two years ago, and now she's leaving England to live with relatives who make their home in the exotic Amazon. Accompanied by her governess, Maia boards a ship and heads to her new life, only to discover it isn't what she had in mind. Suspense, adventure, and plenty of drama await the heroine as she navigates cruelty and injustice.

The Tapir Scientist: Saving South America's Largest Mammal (Brazil)
Sy Montgomery; photographs by Nic Bishop

Journey alongside an award-winning writer and photographer as they make their way to Brazil to track the tapir: a fascinating mammal that looks like a cross between a prehistoric elephant and a hippo. Each chapter describes their daily experiences in the wild as they study this endangered species. Part of the Scientists in the Field Series.

The Walls of Cartagena (Colombia)
Julia Durango; illustrated by Tom Pohrt

Calepino was born on a slave ship while crossing the Atlantic from Angola to Colombia. After his mother dies on board, his future changes in an instant when a Spanish noblewoman decides to raise him. Now the young teen commits to help those whose fate he would have shared, and he hatches a plan to free a mother and son recently sold to a terrible master.

My Havana: Memories of a Cuban Boyhood (Cuba)
Rosemary Wells; illustrated by Peter Ferguson

Young Dino loves "his Havana," and regularly sketches the city's beautiful buildings in his free time. He clings to his drawings and memories of Cuba, even when the family must move to escape dictatorships. In New York City, Dino struggles to feel accepted, but creating a model of Havana on his bedroom floor helps. Based on a true story, this is a good read for children struggling with change.

GLOBAL PERSPECTIVE

How do you give your children the world in your home?

"We recently 'traveled' to Brazil. We looked up videos, music, and read about their primary exports and imports. We researched the religious beliefs and read up on current news in the area. This is typical of how we 'explore' the world, and I always end with the same questions: 'Would you like to live there one day? Why or why not?'" Monica, Tennessee

Where the Flame Trees Bloom (Cuba) | Alma Flor Ada

From Alma Flor Ada comes this lovely collection of eleven autobiographical short stories about her island home. These narratives explore Cuban culture while also showcasing the beauty of human nature: the poor ice-cream vendor who gives out free samples, the grandfather who values people more than things, the blind great-grandmother who never went to school but shares plenty of wisdom, and more.

The Tarantula Scientist (French Guiana)
Sy Montgomery; photographs by Nic Bishop

Another installment in the Scientists in the Field Series, this title invites readers to French Guiana alongside arachnologist Sam Marshall as he searches for tarantulas to study. If you have nature enthusiasts at home, be sure to check out these books!

The Composition (Latin America)
Antonia Skarmeta; illustrated by Alfanso Ruano

Pedro spends most of his free time playing soccer—until the day soldiers arrive and drag away his friend's father. The next morning an officer shows up in Pedro's class to announce that all students must write a paper: What My Parents Do at Night. As Pedro prepares his own essay, he realizes that his words have great power over his family's future. A compelling snapshot of life under a dictatorship.

The Corn Grows Ripe (Latin America)
Dorothy Rhoads—Newbery Honor

Twelve-year-old Tigre has never done a man's work, and his great-grandmother regularly scolds him for laziness. Now his father has been badly injured and the family needs someone to provide for them. Can Tigre put his childish ways behind him and grow the corn they must have to survive? *Note: Mayan religious beliefs mentioned*

The Honey Jar (Latin America)
Rigoberta Menchu; illustrated by Domi

This book compiles twelve Mayan folktales and ancient legends together, including creation tales, fables of the natural world, and stories about the value of hard work. Titles include "The Story of the Weasel Who Helped People Find Corn" and "Grandmother Moon and Grandfather Sun Were Bored." *Note: Mayan religious beliefs mentioned*

Maya: Amazing Inventions You Can Build Yourself (Latin America)
Sheri Bell-Rehwoldt; illustrated by Tom Casteel

A good choice for readers who enjoy history and crafts, *Maya* offers a practical way to study this ancient culture. It includes step-by-step instructions to make common Mayan inventions including calendars, hieroglyphics, musical instruments, and more. *Note: Mayan religious beliefs and practices mentioned, including human sacrifices*

Becoming Naomi Leon (Mexico/U.S.) | Pam Muñoz Ryan

Ever since their mother left seven years ago, Naomi and her brother have lived peacefully with their grandmother in a Californian trailer park. But now their mother suddenly reappears with a new boyfriend and harsh intentions. Gram takes the children to Mexico to find their father and build a case for guardianship.

the way, Naomi begins to discover who she really is, finding courage to confront the obstacles in her path.

Dancing Home (Mexico/U.S.)
Alma Flor Ada & Gabriel M. Zubizarreta

Margie has distanced herself from her Mexican heritage as much as possible, clinging to her American identity to avoid being teased and bullied. Then her cousin Lupe arrives from Mexico and gets assigned to Margie's class, and the girl finds she can no longer run from this side of her life—instead she must embrace it.

The Day It Snowed Tortillas (Mexico/U.S.)
Joe Hayes; illustrated by Antonio Castro Lopez

In this bilingual collection of ten folktales, young readers meet a handful of memorable characters—including those from the author's title story: a foolish woodcutter and his clever wife, who manage to keep a bag of stolen gold after convincing the original robbers that it had recently snowed tortillas. Packed with fun, magic, and a bit of mystery, these are well written and beautifully illustrated.

The Case of the Vanishing Golden Frogs: A Scientific Mystery
(Panama) | Sandra Markle

In the 1990s, the golden frogs of Panama, a national symbol, began to disappear from their usual habitat. When scientists finally found them, the frogs were diseased and dying. What could cause the slow extinction of this species? And how could the scientists protect the remaining frogs? A story sure to interest nature lovers.

Secret of the Andes (Peru) | Ann Nolan Clark—Newbery Medal

Cusi grows up under the care of old man Chuto, a llama herder in the Andes Mountains. Though the Spanish culture is now prominent in Peru, Chuto has raised the boy with traditional Incan ways. Eventually Cusi leaves to find himself, only to uncover an incredible surprise—he is actually Incan royalty.

CHAPTER 12

SAILING OFF: AUSTRALIA, OCEANIA, AND THE POLAR REGIONS

Countries/regions included in this chapter: Antarctica, Arctic, Australia, New Zealand, Papua New Guinea

It's a little ironic. There I was, energetically researching hundreds of books for *Give Your Child the World*, yet sometimes so busy I'd forget to tell my own kids about the cool titles I had found. I'd read a pile of books, write about them, and put them on our designated library shelf where sometimes they'd be picked up and sometimes passed by. Finally I remembered a technique from school—librarians or teachers giving "book talks" to ignite reading interest.

So, taking a stack to the breakfast table one morning, I said, "Before we start our day, I want to show you some new books." I held up each one and gave a short, exciting summary. As I suspected, they were quickly devoured! Use this method to encourage and broaden your kids' reading interests. Make it super-easy on yourself by just reading aloud the back-cover summary. Why not practice book talking with a few titles from this chapter?

BOOKS FOR AGES 4–6

Antarctica Antics: A Book of Penguin Poems (Antarctica)
Judy Sierra; illustrated by Jose Aruego & Ariane Dewey

Perfect for reading aloud, this collection of silly rhyming poems teaches littles plenty about the emperor penguins of Antarctica as the birds swim, eat, play, and stay warm waiting for Mother to return with food.

Lost and Found (Antarctica) | Oliver Jeffers

When a penguin shows up on a boy's doorstep, the only thing to do is help him find his way home. On their way to the South Pole, the boy and the penguin become friends, making it hard to say goodbye . . . so they decide not to. Even my older boys giggled through this one!

Tacky the Penguin (Antarctica)
Helen Lester; illustrated by Lynn Munsinger

Tacky isn't like other penguins. He can't march properly or dive gracefully, and his songs about fish toes don't make sense. But his fellow penguin friends are awfully glad to have Tacky around the day hunters show up. If your young kids love Tacky, look for all the books he stars in!

GLOBAL PERSPECTIVE

How do you give your children the world in your home?

"We have a large map next to our dining room table. We refer to it anytime another culture comes up in TV shows, books, or conversations. We talk about how people live, the geography and wildlife, and what we think it would be like to visit. Sometimes, we take it a step further and watch YouTube videos about it. We are not able to travel much right now, due to one of my son's special needs, but we work for our boys to have a global perspective in any way we can." Shawna, California

Kumak's Fish: A Tall Tale from the Far North (Arctic) | Michael Bania

You've heard that it takes a village to raise a child, but in this case it takes a village to catch a fish! Cooperation, teamwork, and generosity all show up when Kumak's fishing line twitches and he can't reel it in on his own. The villagers refuse to give up and all share in the spoils after their success.

The Little Polar Bear (Arctic) | Hans de Beer

Introduce your kids to Lars, the baby polar bear who lives at the North Pole. This title kicks off an entire series, and in each one Lars has a new adventure sure to delight. In this first installment, the bear's ice breaks apart in the night and he wakes to find himself in the tropics. Sweet and imaginative.

Mama, Do You Love Me? (Arctic)
Barbara Joosse; illustrated by Barbara Lavallee

A young girl tests her independence and her mother to find out just how far their love will stretch. The delightful drawings and text feature many Arctic animals and symbols—all fully explained in an ending glossary. A bedtime story to read again and again.

Over in the Arctic: Where the Cold Winds Blow (Arctic)
Marianne Berkes; illustrated by Jill Dubin

Get ready to sing this picture book, created to the tune of "Over in the Meadow." Each page introduces another Arctic creature—polar bears, hares, wolves—as well as reinforcing numbers and counting. After reading, go back and hunt for "hidden" Arctic animals in the illustrations!

Polar Bear Night (Arctic)
Lauren Thompson; illustrated by Stephen Savage

Follow a baby polar bear as she wakes in her den, slips past her sleeping mother, and heads out for a peek at the still, calm night that "lights up everything she loves." Linocut print artwork complements each carefully chosen word.

Sailing Off to Sleep (Arctic)
Linda Ashman; illustrated by Susan Winter

A little girl isn't quite ready for sleep when bedtime arrives, so instead she charts an adventurous expedition up to the North Pole. After meeting polar bears, caribou, and auks, the girl decides that perhaps home *is* good enough for today. One to cuddle up with.

The Three Snow Bears (Arctic) | Jan Brett

Brett brilliantly recreates the story of Goldilocks in the Arctic with polar bears and an Inuit girl. In the search to find her missing dog team, Aloo-ki stumbles upon an igloo where she eats some soup, tries on boots, takes a nap in a small bed, and wakes just in time to see three pairs of polar bear eyes staring at her. So fun!

The Biggest Frog in Australia (Australia) | Susan L. Roth

Turn these pages and meet the biggest frog in Australia, who wakes up thirsty and proceeds to drink *all* the water, until the earth is dry and the other animals are parched. Wombat, Koala, and others come up with a plan to make the frog laugh so water will flow again. Inspired by an Australian folktale.

Big Rain Coming (Australia)
Katrina Germein; illustrated by Bronwyn Bancroft

On Sunday afternoon, Old Stephen predicts rain—but the downpour doesn't come until the end of the week. Until then, everyone does their best to keep cool. A brightly colored snapshot of Aboriginal culture your little listeners will enjoy.

Diary of a Wombat (Australia)
Jackie French; illustrated by Bruce Whatley

Don't miss this laugh-out-loud read that introduces one of Australia's famous animals. Charming illustrations highlight the wombat's "busy" day of sleeping, eating grass, and scratching! Look for the sequels: *Diary of a Baby Wombat* and *Christmas Wombat*.

Edward the Emu (Australia)
Sheena Knowles; illustrated by Rod Clement

Edward the Emu is sick of being an emu in a zoo and decides to try out other options. He spends one day as a seal, another as a lion, and even one slithering alongside the snakes. But when he returns to his pen, he discovers something that makes him think perhaps being himself isn't all that bad! Also check out *Edwina the Emu*.

Josephine Wants to Dance (Australia)
Jackie French; illustrated by Bruce Whatley

Josephine doesn't care that kangaroos are only supposed to jump—she wants to dance! And when the prima ballerina in town injures her foot before a performance, Josephine gets her big break. Such fun—with guest appearances by several other Australian animals.

Over in Australia: Amazing Animals Down Under (Australia)
Marianne Berkes; illustrated by Jill Dubin

Another installment in the "Over in the Meadow" collection, this one features Australian animals such as wallabies, emus, and brolgas. The afterword shares extra facts about the creatures for little listeners who'd like to learn more.

Possum Magic (Australia) | Mem Fox; illustrated by Julie Vivas

Trying to protect her granddaughter Hush from snakes, Grandma Poss uses bush magic to make the girl possum invisible. But after a while, Hush wants to see herself again, so she and her grandmother set out on a culinary tour of Australia to find the ingredient that will reverse the spell. Also check out Fox's title *Koala Lou*.

Wombat Divine: A Christmas Story from Down Under (Australia)
Mem Fox; illustrated by Kerry Argent

Christmas is Wombat's favorite holiday, and he's been waiting to audition for the nativity play. He's finally old enough this year, yet none of the parts seem right. This title will steal your heart and make your kids belly laugh! *Note: Christian beliefs mentioned*

Wombat Stew (Australia)
Marcia K. Vaughan; illustrated by Pamela Lofts

Dingo has finally caught a wombat and decides to make gooey, brewy, yummy, chewy wombat stew. When Wombat's friends get involved, though, Dingo doesn't realize the kind of stew he's signed up for. Silly and fun.

BOOKS FOR AGES 6–8

A Mother's Journey (Antarctica)
Sandra Markle; illustrated by Alan Marks

Watch a young emperor penguin lay her first egg. Leaving it with her mate, she departs for a five-day journey to the sea. Facing predators and other dangers, the mother must return with food before her baby starves. Also check out *The Emperor's Egg* by Martin Jenkins to get the father penguin's perspective on the same process.

GLOBAL PERSPECTIVE

How do you give your children the world in your home?

"We do it through food! I love to cook and bake, so this gives our family an opportunity to make different recipes from areas that awaken our palate to diversity and an awareness of food items that are not necessarily common to us." Shirley, California

---

Penguin Chick (Antarctica)
Betty Tatham; illustrated by Helen K. Davie

I enjoyed this year-in-the-life tale of an emperor penguin chick, which features charming drawings that highlight the two parents and their baby. The book emphasizes the importance of family, through the nurturing of the mother and father, making it easy for young readers to imagine.

Akiak: A Tale from the Iditarod (Arctic) | Robert J. Blake

Ten-year-old husky Akiak has run the Iditarod three times, yet her team has never won. This year's race is her last chance, but an injury to her paw forces her musher to leave the dog behind. Though it looks as if her hopes for victory have ended, Akiak refuses to give up so easily!

Arctic Son (Arctic)
Jean Craighead George; illustrated by Wendell Minor

At Luke's birth, his Arctic neighbors bestow on him the honor of a traditional name, Kupaaq. The boy grows up in a flat tundra—with polar bears as his nearest companions. The sun doesn't set in summer and doesn't rise in winter. Yet in this land he still plays, works, learns, and loves like children everywhere.

Big Enough Anna: The Little Sled Dog Who Braved the Arctic (Arctic)
Pam Flowers; illustrated by Bill Farnsworth

Based on the true story of the first woman to cross the Arctic alone, *Big Enough Anna* relates the story of the smallest member of the trip—the young but tough puppy chosen to lead the expedition. An inspiring reminder that the strength we have inside can equip us for life's adventures.

The Bravest Dog Ever: The True Story of Balto (Arctic)
Natalie Standiford; illustrated by Donald Cook

On these pages, heroic Balto takes the lead role to deliver life-saving medicine to the children of Nome, Alaska. The dog and his musher travel fifty-three miles through treacherous blizzards to accomplish their mission.

Building an Igloo (Arctic) | Ulli Steltzer
Step-by-step descriptions and photographs offer a detailed look at the igloo-building process. A father and son construct a new house (including a porch) together before preparing for a day of hunting. Fascinating!

North: The Amazing Story of Arctic Migration (Arctic)
Nick Dowson; illustrated by Patrick Benson

We tend to think the Arctic has only one season, but this book shows otherwise. As the weather warms slightly in spring, caribou, geese, whales, and polar bears migrate north, creating a temporary bustle in the barren land. Dreamy watercolors convey the area's sparse beauty.

The Polar Bear Son: An Inuit Tale (Arctic) | Lydia Dabcovich
An old woman relies on the generosity of villagers to survive, until the day she takes in a polar bear cub. As the baby grows, he begins to hunt and fish for his

adoptive mother. Eventually the woman must send her "son" away to keep him safe, but even then their bond remains.

Audrey of the Outback (Australia) | Christine Harris

Audrey is Australia's answer to Pippi Longstocking and Ramona Quimby. The curious girl grows up far from any town or school, without friends her age. She can't play with her younger brother (who only likes to pretend he's a bird) so she turns to her mysterious pet Stumpy. Together they befriend lonely travelers who pass through, accidentally blow up an outhouse, and just have a fine time. *Audrey Goes to Town* and *Audrey's Big Secret* round out the series.

Australia ABCs: A Book about the People and Places of Australia (Australia) | Sarah Heiman; illustrated by Arturo Avila

Did you know that tour groups can actually climb to the top of Harbour Bridge in Sydney? I didn't either until I finished this book's tour. Each page bursts with noteworthy facts about the plants, animals, and people of this unique continent.

The Complete Adventures of Blinky Bill (Australia) | Dorothy Wall

Originally published in the 1930s, this set of stories about a mischievous koala and the bush he lives in has never gone out of print. Loved by Australians for generations, the simple tales also touch on important themes like conservation. *Note: Blinky's father is killed by humans in the first story*

D Is for Down Under: An Australia Alphabet (Australia) Devin Scillian; illustrated by Geoff Cook

This page-by-page excursion around Australia appeals to both younger and older readers. The short rhymes for each letter fit the attention span of little listeners, but detailed sidebars offer extra information for those who'd like to go deeper into the creatures and history of this island continent.

Mirror (Australia) | Jeannie Baker

This wordless picture book follows the daily routine of a boy in Sydney, Australia, and another on the other side of the world in Morocco. In widespread illustrations, *Mirror* reflects the two families' activities—showing that though the cultures differ, many similarities remain. The colorful 3D collages seem to leap off the page!

The Outback (Australia)
Annaliese Porter; illustrated by Bronwyn Bancroft

Your children will be impressed to discover that this book's author wrote it when she was just eight years old! One of Australia's youngest published authors, Porter captures the outback and all its creatures through her poetry paired with images from a well-known Australian illustrator.

GLOBAL PERSPECTIVE

How do you give your children the world in your home?

"We talk about the world every day as well as issues in our own neighborhood, such as refugees coming to our country. My husband and I like the children to know how blessed they are to live in a first-world country, so we often study a day in the life of someone else. We think it's important to be globally aware." Natalie, Australia

---

Where the Forest Meets the Sea (Australia) | Jeannie Baker

A boy and his father adventure to the Australian rain forest for a trip back in time—remembering the people and animals that made their homes there. Ancient creatures like dinosaurs even begin to emerge from hiding in the boy's imagination. The sparse text fits the 4–6 age range, but the final warning about rain-forest destruction makes it a better fit for ages 6–8.

Elizabeth: Queen of the Seas (New Zealand)
Lynne Cox; illustrated by Brian Floca

Meet Elizabeth, the elephant seal named after the Queen of England, who makes her home in the Avon River of Christchurch, New Zealand. When she tries to sun herself on a busy road, residents become concerned and tow her out to sea. But this seal knows where she belongs. I love the photograph of the real Elizabeth at the end!

BOOKS FOR AGES 8-10

Ann and Liv Cross Antarctica (Antarctica)
Zoe Alderfer Ryan; illustrated by Nicholas Reti

Ann and Liv have an outlandish goal—to be the first women to cross Antarctica. After years of planning and training, the pair departs on their dangerous trek. They only have one hundred days before conditions become impassable. The pages encourage readers to come up with their own bold dreams.

Ice Wreck (Antarctica) | Lucille Recht Penner

This beginning chapter book captures the thrill of Ernest Shackleton's expedition. It also focuses on his wisdom and sacrifice as a leader—giving his sleeping bag to another sailor and taking the most dangerous jobs himself. The eight- to ten-year-old group will enjoy this title on their own, but it could also make a good read-aloud for younger children.

Mr. Popper's Penguins (Antarctica) | Richard & Florence Atwater

While it's true that most of Mr. Popper's Penguins does not take place in Antarctica, this laugh-out-loud story of a painter with a passion is too precious to be skipped! Mr. Popper's love for his penguins and the polar regions is contagious and can easily lead to an in-depth unit study on the area and the birds.

Penguins (Antarctica) | Seymour Simon

Published in conjunction with Smithsonian, Penguins takes readers on an adventurous trek to Antarctica to answer questions like "How can penguins be birds if they can't fly?" Stunning photos capture their entire life cycle—from the hatching of their eggs to social traditions and dangerous predators.

Shackleton's Journey (Antarctica) | William Grill

This version of Shackleton's tale has incredible colored pencil drawings and goes in-depth into the exploration before it started (how did they choose twenty-six men out of the five thousand who applied?), during the journey, and even afterward, when Shackleton returned to help rescue another party. Any young explorer in your home will be drawn to this exciting depiction!

Sophie Scott Goes South (Antarctica) | Alison Lester

Nine-year-old Sophie travels from Australia to Antarctica with her father, captain of an icebreaker. The girl keeps track of her experiences in journal entries, which make up the bulk of the text. So much to take in on these pages: diagrams, photos, facts about early explorers. Plenty to keep young readers engaged.

Trapped by the Ice! (Antarctica) | Michael McCurdy

Written sequentially, this picture book begins in 1915 with Shackleton's *Endurance* trapped in the ice and ends in 1916 when the explorer finally reaches help at a nearby island. Definitely an engrossing, dramatic read-aloud!

Balto and the Great Race (Arctic) | Elizabeth Cody Kimmel

This chapter book version of Balto's trip to Nome, Alaska, to save sick children will keep your dog lovers thrillingly engaged. Reading it made me want to visit New York City's Central Park and see the dog's statue, which still honors his courageous trek.

I, Matthew Henson: Polar Explorer (Arctic)
Carole Boston Weatherford; illustrated by Eric Velasquez

Explorer Matthew Henson overcame prejudice and lifelong obstacles to make history at the North Pole. Written in verse from Henson's perspective, readers come away from this story with a sense of the explorer's courage and his refusal to let racism hold him back. If Henson inspires your children, also check out *Keep On!: The Story of Matthew Henson* by Deborah Hopkinson.

Ookpik: The Travels of a Snowy Owl (Arctic) | Bruce Hiscock

Follow the first year of Ookpik's life as he hatches, is fed by his parents, then launches into hunting and migrating. Passing from the Arctic through Canada and into the United States, Ookpik spends the winter delighting bird lovers before heading home again in the spring.

Togo (Arctic) | Robert J. Blake

Togo's owner plans to use him as a pet instead of a sled dog, but Togo never got the memo. Instead, his energy lands him at the front of a life-or-death situation—when serum is needed to stop the diphtheria epidemic of Nome, Alaska. You may have heard of the brave dog Balto; now meet the animal that made Balto's journey possible.

GLOBAL PERSPECTIVE

How do you give your children the world in your home?

"Little Passports is a joy for our boys, we subscribe to Compassion magazine, and have regular conversations about what life is like in different places (the good and bad). We learn phrases from other languages and have an international food night once a week. The food leads to many questions: Where does this come from? What are these spices? How are they grown?" Kristin, North Carolina

Australia and Oceania | Mel Friedman

This nonfiction volume packs a full load of facts about the countries down under into a handful of colorful pages. It introduces readers to engaging tidbits like homeschooling in the Outback, the popular mining of Australian opals, and the history of "criminals" being sent to the continent for stealing a loaf of bread.

Bright Star (Australia) | Gary Crew; illustrated by Anne Spudvilas

Alicia, a farm girl in nineteenth-century Australia, is bored by the traditional roles forced on her—needlework, chores, cooking. She dreams of space and longs to study the stars. When a local astronomer comes to Alicia's school and encourages her to visit his observatory, she gets her first inspiring glimpse of the heavens.

Marsupials (Australia) | Nic Bishop

Bishop's stunning snapshots hop Australia's creatures right off the pages in this guide to the world's marsupials. A few entries mention other continents as well, but Bishop mainly focuses on his six months in Australia. I loved the ending in which he shares the secrets he uses to coax animals near enough to photograph.

This Is Australia (Australia) | Miroslav Sasek

Sasek's geographical trips around the world continue with this volume on Australia. Originally written in the 1970s, some of the book's information may seem dated, but it includes revised statistics at the end. The charming illustrations and details on the cities, architecture, and animals of the island will keep your readers engaged.

BOOKS FOR AGES 10–12

Fatty Legs: A True Story (Arctic)
Christy Jordan-Fenton & Margaret Pokiak-Fenton

Olemaun wants to learn to read and not even the fear of leaving her Arctic village for the nearby government school dissuades her. When Olemaun arrives at the school, though, a harsh nun renames the girl "Margaret" and singles her out to humiliate. But Olemaun knows who she is and stands up to the injustice. A moving memoir. *Note: Catholic nuns at the school treat children cruelly*

Ice Drift (Arctic) | Theodore Taylor

Can Alika and Sulu survive six months lost in the Arctic? That's the question that will keep tweens reading as these two Inuit brothers face dangers such as polar bears and melting ice floes in their quest to return home to their father safely. *Note: Inuit religious beliefs mentioned*

The Igloo (Arctic) | Charlotte & David Yue

This detailed book contains chapters covering every aspect of Inuit culture: igloo building; family life; roles for men, women, and children; hunting and food preparation; and community. The black-and-white illustrations and diagrams kept me intrigued—I learned so much just flipping through its pages. *Note: Inuit religious beliefs mentioned*

The Snow Baby: The Childhood of Admiral Robert E. Peary's Daring Daughter (Arctic) | Katherine Kirkpatrick

Kids who love adventure will gravitate toward this real-life daring childhood account of Marie Peary, daughter of the first explorer to reach the North Pole. Born in the Arctic, she grows up with Inuit children as her best friends and polar animals as her pets. Fascinating black-and-white photos!

Hitler's Daughter (Australia) | Jackie French

Mark's friend Anna makes up stories to pass the time while waiting for the school bus in their Australian neighborhood. But this morning her imaginary tale ventures into unknown territory: it's about Hitler's daughter. As Anna continues her saga, Mark starts to wonder . . . "If someone close to me was doing wrong, would I be able to tell?" This novel easily segues into further study about Holocaust survivors as well as the Aborigines.

Jodie's Journey (Australia) | Colin Thiele

Jodie loves riding her horse Monarch. She spends every spare moment preparing for competitions with him, until the day that a strange pain spreads across her body. Eventually diagnosed with rheumatoid arthritis, Jodie must face reality: she will never compete again. An inspiring story of meeting life's unexpected challenges.

My Place (Australia) | Nadia Wheatley & Donna Rawlins

This picture book details Australia's history over a two-hundred-year period by following a single piece of land and time's transformation of it. Each two-page spread highlights one decade and one child on the land, going all the way back to the Aborigines. Readers will love the many maps and details.

GLOBAL PERSPECTIVE

How do you give your children the world in your home?

"Prior to having children, we were missionaries with Youth with a Mission, so worldview is an important part of our life and education. We are unable to physically travel at this time, but we keep a globe next to our table. We use world-focused curriculum and talk about other cultures and lifestyles. We haven't started learning foreign languages yet, but intend to in the future." Hannah, United Kingdom

Seven Little Australians (Australia) | Ethel Turner

The Australian equivalent of *Cheaper by the Dozen*, this book from the late 1800s shares the trials and mischiefs of the seven Woolcot children—along with their domineering father and young stepmother. Don't expect deep lessons from this read—it is mostly full of playful pranks kids can relate to. But also be aware that like *Cheaper*, it has a sad ending worth previewing first.

The Silver Brumby (Australia) | Elyne Mitchell

A classic of Australian fiction, this is a sure-to-please title for the adventure lovers and horse lovers in your home. A silver brumby is an exquisite, magical stallion—widely hunted by both humans and other horses. Thowra, King of the Brumbies, must defend his herd against savage beasts and men. *The Silver Brumby* is the start of a series, with ten other books following it.

Sun on the Stubble (Australia) | Colin Thiele

Twelve-year-old Bruno's stern father orders him off the farm and to the nearest school a town away. Leaving home sends Bruno on a trip down memory lane, recalling all his past escapades: catching possums and criminals, building dams across the creek, and dodging trouble when possible. Each chapter stages a different episode in the boy's life, making for a fun read-aloud.

Tom Appleby, Convict Boy (Australia) | Jackie French

After his father dies in a British prison, eight-year-old Tom gets caught stealing bread. The punishment? Deportation to prison in Botany Bay. But the boy catches a lucky break soon after his arrival, when a sergeant takes him on as a servant. Together they build a house, plant a garden, and watch as the country comes alive from the ground up.

Where in the World (Australia) | Simon French

Ari lost his father at the age of three, but his musical grandfather and violin have always seen him through tough times. Now his mother has decided to move to Australia, and Ari must leave his Opa and again deal with loss and grief. In the process, he learns to let music heal his pain—and summons the courage to share his gift with others.

The Quest for the Tree Kangaroo: An Expedition to the Cloud Forest of New Guinea (Papua New Guinea)
Sy Montgomery; illustrated by Nic Bishop

Enthusiasm for science and nature crawls across the pages of this title as readers follow a biologist to Papua New Guinea in search of the rare Matschie tree kangaroo. A combination of a bear, a monkey, and a kangaroo, scientists track it through the cloud forest to learn about and protect it. Also look for *Kakapo Rescue: Saving the World's Strangest Parrot* and head to New Zealand with the same team.

HOW TO RAISE A
WORLD-CHANGER

We tend to overcomplicate parenting these days, an approach that leads to unnecessary stress and overwhelm. So as you finish *Give Your Child the World* and decide how to use it in your family, I wanted to send you off with a final reminder of how simple it can be to raise a child who loves both books and the world.

Enjoy this world and those who journey through it by your side—be blessed!

I haven't met you yet, but I know you're special.
We count down the days 'til you join us,
your room full of anticipation:
Books in one corner, diapers in another.

You're here! And you make your presence known
more each day—your eyes take it all in.
They even watch me dare to start a new book,
then fall asleep, the title forgotten on my chest.

On the move now, no one can stop you!
You explore so much—including the bookshelves.
Once neatly organized, you make them your own:
books in the mouth, books piled in stacks on the floor.

As a preschooler, you open the cover and find the joy.
They don't make sense yet, these shapes on paper,
but on my lap we share one book, then another.
The world grows bigger with each page turned.

No longer content to just listen,
you're on a mission to conquer the letters yourself.
It's painful at times, the slow sounding out,
but after your first sentence, you glow with pride.

An independent reader, it's hard to keep up with you.
The titles fly off the library shelves.
You grab a stack, head to your room,
falling in love with the world before my eyes.

You're ready now, to understand the planet's heartache.
Books give us a front-row seat to wars, loss, overcoming.
Bold and courageous, inspired to action,
selfless dreams and ideas root inside and grow.

My prayer for you, now and forever:
that the world will never lose its wonder,
that you may always have an open book in hand,
and an open heart within, to learn and apply its lessons.

You're a world-changer, dear child, and the world is waiting for what only you can give.

ACKNOWLEDGMENTS

Give Your Child the World has been a work in progress for over five years. The fact that you now hold it in your hands is a testimony to the power of miracles, the power of baby steps, and the power of incredible friends and family.

A heartfelt hug and deep thanks goes to my amazing literary agent, Jenni Burke of D.C. Jacobson, who saw something in this book that no one else did at the time, and who kept believing in it even when it took longer than expected to find its ideal publishing home.

Thank you, Sandy Vander Zicht of Zondervan, for providing that ideal publishing home and for making this book its absolute best. I've learned so much from your editorial guidance and insight. I deeply appreciate everyone at Zondervan working behind the scenes to get *Give Your Child the World* into as many hands as possible.

Tsh Oxenreider, you took a wild chance years ago when you asked me to help bring Simple Homeschool to life. Thank you for trusting me with such a gift, which has opened doors to so many good things. And to the rest of the original SLM ladies: Kara, Aimee, Nicole, Katie, Mandi, and Arianne. You guys supported me through joyful times and dark days. Forever grateful.

Thank you, Kara Anderson, for freeing me up from blogging so I could concentrate on these words. I know I need never worry when Simple Homeschool is safe in your hands. And perhaps I should also thank Panera for the buckets of iced tea that fuel our work!

LeVar Burton: During the summer of 1985, I rode my bike every morning to Mary C. Williams Elementary School library in Wilmington, North Carolina. I read for a few hours, then pedaled home again in time for back-to-back *Reading Rainbow* episodes. That summer turned me into a lifelong reader—thank you for decades of inspired work.

Caroline Starr Rose, thanks for making me do the ugly cry when I opened the cover of *Blue Birds* and saw my name written there! I'm blessed to have in you the depth of friendship that Kimi and Alis share. Can't wait for us to discover the land that Maud loved together.

This book never would have been possible without the staff at Cyrenius H. Booth Library in Newtown, Connecticut. A special thanks to Candice and Mimi, who helped me get my hands on hundreds of books and never complained.

Mom, thanks for those trips to the library every third Monday. Thanks for not laughing at me (even when I wanted to sleep in a hammock), and for believing in my crazy dreams. Dad, I trust you have a front-row seat to all this, so you can see that those trips in the Celica ended up meaning so much more. Miss you—I can't wait to catch up on the other side. Thanks and love to Nana, Sugie, Tara, Renee, and the rest of my Wilmington family. To Dave, Julie, and the British side: Thank you for welcoming a full-blooded American into the fold years ago. I've been truly blessed with family on both sides of the pond.

Melissa Massett, thank you for sharing your house and heart with me. From Mt. Daniel to Newtown—who could have predicted it?! Jill Turner, thanks for your friendship, your family, and the helpful research you did in the early stages of this book's life. Here's to many homeschooling conferences in our future!

I want to express special thanks to Oliver and Rachel DeMille, for outlining the educational philosophy that has brought so much richness to our family life. I'm also deeply grateful, Rachel, for your wise and gracious responses to the desperately sent Mommy emails I throw your way now and then.

Readers of Simple Homeschool and Steady Mom: This book wouldn't have a life if it weren't for you. Your courage to parent, learn, and teach outside the box inspires me daily, and gets me out of bed to scribble away each morning. Thank you!

Steve, it's a good thing hardworking 3's and sensitive 4's go so well together. You sacrificed to make this book happen, listened to me whine when it felt too hard, and believed in me when I no longer believed in myself. I can't wait to see what happens next. With you by my side, it's guaranteed to be an adventure. Love you.

Kids: Mommy found her life's work and a new calling through the three of you. Trishna, thank you for always calling me "clever and creative." Jonathan, thank you for loving books as much as I do. Elijah, thank you for all the hugs, back rubs, and prayers. All of you see me at my best and worst and love me anyway. What a miracle to walk life's road alongside you. Only God could have put our family together, and he deserves all my thanks and love, now and forever.

NOTES

CHAPTER 1: THE GOOD EARTH: A LOVE STORY

1. Anne Lamott, *Bird by Bird* (New York: Anchor Books, 1994), 186.

CHAPTER 2: PRACTICAL WAYS TO INVITE THE WORLD INTO YOUR HOME

2. Sarah Klein, "8 Reasons to Make Time for Family Dinner," *CNN*, October 25, 2011, http://www.cnn.com/2011/10/25/living/family-dinner-h/.

CHAPTER 3: THE POWER OF STORY

3. Debbie Elliot, "'Terabithia' Inspired by True Events," *NPR*, February 18, 2007, http://www.npr.org/templates/story/story.php?storyId=7387562.
4. Jim Trelease, *The Read-Aloud Handbook* (New York: Penguin, 2013), 32.
5. Charlotte Mason, *Home Education* (Radford, VA: Wilder Publications, 2008), 126.

CHAPTER 4: THE JOY OF OTHER LANDS: HOW TO USE THE READING LISTS

6. Oliver and Rachel DeMille, *Leadership Education: The Phases of Learning* (Cedar City: TJED.org, 2008), 35.
7. C. S. Lewis. *Of Other Worlds: Essays and Stories* (San Diego: Harvest Books, 1966), 15.

AUTHOR INDEX

COUNTRY/ REGION INDEX

MULTICULTURAL

HISTORICAL INDEX

TITLE INDEX

CONNECT WITH JAMIE

For more book recommendations and out-of-the-box thoughts on parenting and education, visit Jamie's blogs: SimpleHomeschool.net and SteadyMom.com.

ABOUT LOVE146

The trafficking of children is one of the darkest stories and most severe human rights abuses imaginable. But the hope of ending it is a reality. Love146 is an international human rights organization working to end child trafficking and exploitation through survivor care and prevention.

Find out more and join the movement at love146.org.